The Fabric We Make

How to Knit a Community

by Joe Wilcox

Dedication

Edward Myatt (1959-2022), or KnitterGuy Ted, was exceptionally talented at creating intricate and beautiful knitted fabric. Many of us in the knitting community have benefited from his vast knowledge and experience. He also left an important legacy by establishing the Men's Knitting Retreats. The foundational goals and intentions he set in place for the retreats continue to foster and celebrate a most amazing community.

Introduction

A corporate performance review of my work once stated that "Joe gravitates toward the more enjoyable aspects of his job." I loved this evaluation because it was both succinct and true. It was meant as a criticism. My boss intended to infer that I neglected the less enjoyable aspects of my job. I saw it more as an accurate description of my general philosophy. Gravitating towards joy has led me on a wonderfully unexpected journey of finding out not only who I am, but the exact kind of community that pushes me further toward that joy as well.

Having a deep sense of belonging to a community can be a rare and transformative experience, especially when a community emerges unexpectedly. I have seen communities form in response to a dire need. I've also seen communities form and solidify when a new group comes together and the members are so enthused by coming together that they become determined to have the group persist. Regardless of how a stable community forms, the sense of belonging it elicits is profoundly satisfying. The unexpected and spontaneous formation of such a community can be an exuberant experience for all those involved.

I am a gay knitter in a long-term relationship who has blogged about knitting and queer issues since 2002 under the online moniker of QueerJoe. I also helped found the Men's Knitting Retreats, an organization that has regularly scheduled retreats since 2008 celebrating the community of men who knit, crochet, weave – anything to do with yarn and fiber. Readers of my blog already know that I often express myself with sometimes blunt directness. This book isn't intended to persuade or sway you to think differently about any particular issue. It is simply to offer what I hope will be useful history and insight about this most unusual and unexpected community of which I've become a part. Documenting and conjecturing about what has been a transformative experience from an unlikely confluence of circumstances, is my only agenda.

The first time I was deeply moved by an experience of belonging was when my partner Thaddeus and I visited San Francisco. It was 1989 and we stayed with a friend who lived there. As I walked around the gay sections of the city, I realized that for the first time in my adult life, I wasn't a minority. We were in a place where gay men were the norm. Being in public where just the act of holding my partner's hand wasn't considered a political statement, was joyous and freeing. I could feel my shoulders relax when I hadn't even realized they had ever been tense. This first sense of being a part of a community, rather than an outsider, sparked in me the desire to seek out similar situations where I felt as though I truly belonged.

I have spoken about this experience to other members of the queer community who have nodded in complete understanding. I'm sure there are many similar versions of this experience for anyone who has been made to feel as "other" - not a part of their everyday society - and who suddenly found themselves in a place where they belonged for the first time.

I was raised in a large, loving family with six siblings and have always felt a sense of belonging. I never imagined there could be a sense of not belonging. When I began to realize that I might be different from other boys, I somehow determined that my differences were to be kept hidden. My three older brothers were into sports, both as participants and spectators. I had neither aptitude nor interest in sports, even though it was clear that the norm was for boys to both like and compete in sports. Trying to fit in, I joined the farm team of the Little League baseball club and spent endless, boring hours out in left field hoping no balls would be hit in my direction. I also much preferred spending time with my younger sister and her friends than my older brothers and their friends. In my teens, I started to have feelings that I had been conditioned to believe were wrong. My church, my family and my friends had all made it clear that guys shouldn't be attracted to other guys and if you were, you should hide it.

When I was in San Francisco and found myself in an environment where there was no need to conceal my thoughts and actions from others, it showed me just how much I had adapted to keep that part of myself hidden. Not only did it show me how much I had adapted, but it also allowed me to notice all the protective behaviors that weren't necessary when I felt like I was in a safer environment. It felt like taking off layers of heavy clothing. I felt a floating lightness and the freedom was intoxicating. Although, the only "outrageous" thing I did to celebrate was walk through the streets with my arm around Thaddeus.

A very different spontaneous community was one that formed miraculously when dire circumstances demanded it. It was in the mid-1980's. Up until this point the acronym LGBTQ hadn't been coined nor had the word "queer" been broadly reclaimed as a title of pride. There had been regular pride protests and marches since the Stonewall riots in 1969 which brought together gay men, lesbians and some of the people in the intersex, non-binary and trans spectrum. But in truth, we were anything but a cohesive community. My experience as a gay man during those years was that there was little in common between gay men and lesbians. There was even less in common with those in the transvestite/transsexual/drag/cross-dressing communities. There was a distinct divide between gay men and lesbians and in all honesty, there was quite a bit of outright disdain for those who would become known as the trans community in those days. Regretfully, it was a lot easier to focus on our differences and remain as separate groups. There were few reasons to join forces and be part of a larger community except perhaps for political power, which didn't seem overly important to me as a young, entitled, white, cis-gendered man. Especially someone who could pass as straight when it benefitted me.

Up until this point, gay and bisexual men and women and members of the transgender, non-binary and intersex community had not yet realized that they shared a big overlap in the Venn diagram of our lives - the fact that we were all considered "other" because we didn't conform to society's gender norms. But soon, something would come along that would change the way we understood and appreciated one another.

In the mid-1980's, AIDS was beginning to decimate the gay male population. Men all around us were getting sick and dying at rates that had us terrified. We were paralyzed by the speed, the confusion, the grief, and the fear of all that was happening. The disease was forcing more and more young men to come out as gay to their families, and many found themselves sick, dying, and disowned. I heard countless stories about dying men whose parents had rejected them, and then after they had died, the parents came back to take all their possessions from surviving partners. When families-of-origin turned their backs on their sons, many times the only people who were helping care for very sick and dying men were their slightly less sick and dying partners.

Health organizations made it harder for many of us rather than easier - especially in the earlier days of the disease when it wasn't certain how AIDS was being transmitted. Out of ignorance, fear and/or bigotry doctors and hospitals were blocking medical care to people with AIDS. Even if they were admitted to a hospital, AIDS patients often experienced less-than-adequate care, and were sometimes outright neglected due to the ignorance and homophobia of the medical staff.

As an individual, I felt paralyzed by the enormity of it all. I volunteered for a newly formed AIDS organization in New Jersey called Hyacinth. I became the volunteer supervisor for their call-in support center. It seemed like a meager effort, one that left me feeling rather helpless and ineffective. When someone called in, there was little support or help I could offer. We had a large Rolodex of agencies, clinics and public accommodations that would help people with AIDS, but it was woefully insufficient for what was needed at such an urgent time. I'll never forget how hopeless I felt when we could only find one funeral home in the entire county where I lived that was willing to take our deceased friends and loved ones who had died of AIDS. It was truly a frightening and lonely time.

That's where the miracle of spontaneous community happened.

Despite historically unwelcoming behaviors on the part of many gay men, and even though they were some of the least infected by HIV, the lesbian community decided that we were, in fact, all one community. They made AIDS our communal cause. They fought, and supported and loved and grieved and helped in every possible way you could imagine. They ran major programs at Hyacinth and other AIDS support organizations. They organized marches, protests, acts of civil disobedience, set up Reiki healing circles, established phone lists of doctors, hospitals, dentists and caretakers who would help us. Lesbian doctors, nurses and social workers recognized our desperate situation and responded to it with equal levels of urgency and incredible amounts of caring. They took charge and brought much-needed leadership to a dire situation. These amazing women pulled us together into what would soon be called the LGBT community. I felt both shame and relief about all they did. Shame, in that I'm not sure I would have championed a similar effort if the roles had been reversed, and the most amazing sense of relief that I was part of a supportive community helping fight against the disease and all the oppression it revealed. I'm not sure how shame and relief added up to gratitude, but being grateful was the overarching emotion and continues to be today.

This is a simplified and personal view of what happened during that time. Out of despair and crisis, a more cohesive and powerful community emerged than had existed up to that point. We were forced to recognize that we needed to rely on each other and focus on what we had in common rather than how we differed. I will be forever grateful for the lesbian community's heroic efforts that saved untold numbers of lives. Their actions helped us understand the vital importance of all human rights and the power of community to help assure that we gained and kept those rights.

The idea of this book started when a specific combination of circumstances created a similarly unexpectedly magical community. There was no crisis or despair that brought this community together. In fact, ever since this community came together, I have been trying to understand exactly what happened in a way that helps to consistently and reliably repeat the experience.

The following chapters will hopefully convey both the circumstances that led up to the community-creating event as well as some of the questions I came up with along the way. Is the formation of community something that simply occurs through mere happenstance? Is it similar to how life emerged from the primordial soup in some unexplained, random way? Does a group form organically and naturally because of some instinctual pull toward each other and remain solidly together like bonded atoms whose protons and electrons matched harmoniously to form an element?

Or is it with great care and deliberate attention that a community forms? Does it require some master sculptor to carve out each component and individual detail? Does a community require someone who carefully picks out and matches each member like some universal matchmaker to form the perfect blend of members?

In my experience, it's somewhere in between those two scenarios. Members of a would-be affinity group or a like-minded community often remain separate. There can be some mild gravitational pull toward each other, but it's usually not strong enough to coalesce them by itself. While they may have occasional interactions with each other, they are usually awaiting some catalyst that will bring them together and bond them in some form of solid community. And once brought together, successful communities often present an individual among their ranks who will be inspired to help foster this community to further unify and grow.

Regardless of how community forms, when it does, it is often a profoundly impactful event in the members' experiences, or at least it is in the communities that last. The "coming together" seems both momentous and magical. When you hear someone state, "I've found my people," it's often the indicator that an unexpected and persistent community is taking root. Or has already taken root and is exerting more gravitational pull as its population of members increases.

Members' feelings about transformative events like the unexpected formation of community can sometimes be both intense and fleeting for the individuals involved. Even a profound, communal experience can have a way of fading into a mere fond memory. At these times intensely felt events are dismissed as being not as impactful as they really were. This is where someone within the community is needed to reinforce and remind and re-create the experience of the initial coalition. At least at the onset, a community needs a guide or a leader to champion the fledgling group.

It took me decades to learn enough about yarn, stitch design, garment structure, fabric drape and color to understand the basic components of a stable and successful knitted project. It took me a similar amount of time to understand the components of a stable and successful community. My experience is that at least three components are necessary to establish community. Individuals with similar interests, with at least a mild gravitational pull toward each other, a catalyst to bring the group together, and a shepherd or shepherds to foster it and encourage it to persist. One other common component is that the similarly-interested, would-be members of a community usually also feel like outsiders in some way.

As with any knitting project, I can have beautiful yarn, a perfect pattern, and years of skill and tools, and still, the project doesn't work out as I'd have hoped. It requires perseverance and sustained effort to successfully create something amazing. Similarly, when all the components of a community are in place, the creation of an amazing community is not assured. But when a wondrous community does form, the group becomes important to the individuals that make up the group. The community establishes itself as an important method of self-identification for its members. The group persona becomes an integral part of each member's personal self-identification.

My experiences of chance meetings with other people who gave me a taste for the comfort and joy of being among my own people, continue to be something profound to me and to the groups I've become a part of. I was able to see an emerging trend of some gravitational pull of people with common interests who were looking for an opportunity to coalesce. Perhaps less clear is whether I've even now reached a culmination in this search for being among my own kind. But I can confidently state that I have found my people and I find that I strongly identify as a member of this group and take much pride in being a member.

Designing and creating a knitted garment for the first time can take considerable amounts of time, creativity and effort. So, when it is a success, we make sure to write up a pattern for this new and beautiful design. At the beginning of this journey, I had no way of knowing that I would be presented with an extraordinary group of like-minded people and a design idea to create a community. I didn't realize yet that I yearned to be among others who felt the same way I did. But for many of us, it was more of an unconscious yearning that we wouldn't understand until we had actually experienced it. We were willing to dedicate time, creativity and effort to see if we could make it a successful design.

Chapter 1
Establishing Identity

*"Never mind searching for who you are.
Search for the person you aspire to be."*

Robert Brault

The memory of the first time I felt compelled to learn to knit is still incredibly vivid. I was 27 years old, and I was at my friend Ernie's house who was living in his parents' basement. Ernie was a know-it-all. Not that kind of know-it-all. He really did seem to know an enormous amount about a surprisingly vast number of topics. For example, we'd have a cracked tile in our bathroom and Ernie would tell us that the color of the tile was Egyptian Gray and that it was no longer being made by the tile manufacturer. Or I'd pick up a nut from a tree and not only would Ernie know that it was a hickory nut, but he'd also know that it was a good year for hickory nuts – that the squirrels hadn't taken them and hidden them for winter as in prior years. Then he'd go on to tell me how to best extract the nut and use it in a praline-like candy recipe. He had a surprising abundance of information on a surprisingly wide variety of topics.

Ernie's mom was into a lot of different crafts and stored most of her crafting supplies in a space behind Ernie's bed. Cake decorating, wreath making, quilting, flower arranging and various fiber crafts were stashed in an alcove behind where Ernie slept. They were somewhat hidden behind a drape which formed a quasi-wall, sectioning off the bedroom from the craft storage. On this particular day, I noticed a small plastic package sticking out from underneath this draped fabric. The package text indicated that it contained a set of four Susan Bates, blue aluminum, double-pointed knitting needles.

I picked them up and asked Ernie what they were and he explained that they were knitting needles. I asked him why there were four of them instead of two, and why they didn't have the typical capped-off ends. While he wasn't a knitter, he was able to explain how this type of needle was used to knit tubular fabric for socks or mittens. Even more clearly, he explained how three of the needles overlapped to form a closed triangle with knit stitches hanging below them in spiraling rounds that created this kind of tubular fabric.

I recognize that most people wouldn't have been overly inspired by this interaction. But for some reason, I was absolutely fascinated. The fact that these simple tools could be used to actually create fabric was revelatory to me. I could clearly see it in my mind the way that Ernie described it.

I remember thinking, "I must find out how to do this!"

Ernie left me alone in his bedroom/craft storage area to help his dad with a task. I quickly put the set of double-pointed needles in my pocket and looked through his mom's pile of knitting pamphlets and pocketed one that looked like it had instructions for knitting socks. For years I told myself that I was just borrowing (without asking) these items. But in the thirty-some-odd years since, they have never been returned. I still try to justify this borrowing/theft by honestly telling myself that I'd be thrilled to let anyone borrow/steal any of my knitting tools or books if they were as excited about knitting as I was.

Fortunately, one of the booklets that I took home had basic how-to knitting instructions with diagrams. It showed how to cast on, knit, purl and bind off, as well as some other useful pictorial instructions. As it turns out, the four techniques (cast on, knit, purl and bind off) are all that a knitter really needs to know. This was well before the internet and YouTube video tutorials. The very next Saturday, I walked a few miles to the Woolworths (a now-defunct department store) in my town which was the only place I knew of that sold yarn. Not knowing anything about knitting or yarn weights, I purchased a couple of skeins of aqua-colored, acrylic yarn and a pair of straight knitting needles and walked back home and taught myself to knit. Despite some minor setbacks, I was able to start creating knitted fabric relatively quickly.

Many of the people I've met over the years who have taught themselves a yarn-craft have a similar story. There was something that seemed to compel them to learn how to make fabric. Even the people who were encouraged to do yarn work by a parent, relative or friend were most likely similarly inspired at one point to want to continue for some unidentifiably compelling reason.

But what cemented the idea for me of becoming a knitter?

It was in the mid-1980's and I had been in a committed relationship for about 3 years with Thaddeus, the man who would eventually become my husband. I was 27 years old and not at all astute about life. But I had a lot of enthusiasm and even more energy. My career was just beginning. I was working in Human Resources at a large banking corporation in New York City and commuting in and out of the city each day. Working on my career wasn't overly engaging for me yet. So, I threw most of my overflow of energy into my relationship with Thaddeus. My ideas about relationships were naïve, to say the least. With Thaddeus working in retail sales, our schedules didn't sync up very well. I worked banker's hours and his job in retail had him working many evenings and weekends. So, wrapping my life around my partner's life started to feel a little bit like I was becoming the hole in his donut - in that without him, there wasn't anything to define me.

I started to ask the age-old question, "Who am I?" Simple questions such as, "What did I like?", "What did I enjoy doing?", "What aspects of my personality did I want to highlight and which did I want to let go of?" all confounded me. I honestly had no idea who I was or what I wanted in life. I wouldn't call it an identity crisis, as I didn't consider it a crisis at all. It was more as though I'd found some gap in who I was that needed to be addressed.

While I may well have been asking the right questions, I didn't have a lot of answers. So, I decided to just start making it up. There wasn't a formal list, but I started to make decisions that began to define who I was. I'd find myself declaring, "I don't like cranberry juice!" or "I'm going to the local bookstore and start reading gay authors." One of those stakes I put firmly in the ground was the statement, "I am a knitter."

That last one might seem an odd choice. I didn't know any knitters except for Ernie's mom and even she was more of a dabbler in all crafts. She wasn't a dedicated knitter. Like most people back then, I thought knitting was relegated to grandmotherly types. So, declaring myself a knitter looked on the outside a bit random.

But the questioning of my identity and the fascination with creating tubular fabric both came at around the same time. I had also had enough experience with gender non-conforming behavior by that point in my life that it never occurred to me that I couldn't get past the gender and age stereotypes. Thaddeus didn't seem to have an issue with my newfound hobby. In fact, he was then, and continues to be extremely supportive. Even if he had taken issue with it, I don't think I could have been dissuaded. Even after just three years together, he recognized that when I got an idea stuck in my head, no matter how illogical it was, I was going to pursue it.

This deliberate forming of my personal identity seemed to have two effects. First, it was giving more solid form to this amorphous idea of who I was. I was starting to distinguish myself as a distinct individual. I imagine that most people go through this process, but I'm not sure if most people make quite so mindful of a choice about it. The second effect of declaring who I was, was that I began to notice aspects of my newfound identity in my day-to-day life.

A friend once told me the story about how one autumn when the trees in the Northeast of the U.S. were starting to change color, they were disappointed that they weren't seeing any vibrant red trees. But almost by magic, just the utterance of those words, red-leaf trees started showing up in their life. Big, bright red-leafed trees were now almost everywhere. Were those trees there all the time? Yes, of course they were. The words of disappointment didn't speak the trees into existence. But those same words did start to bring red trees into conscious awareness.

Similarly, declaring myself a knitter, I started to see knitter things. Pharmacies that sold magazines had knitting magazines on their racks! There were even some women's magazines that published special annual knitting issues. I came to realize that there were entire stores devoted to selling yarn and knitting tools. Yard sales and flea markets often had knitting paraphernalia to be purchased inexpensively. Woolworths wasn't the only place to buy these skeins of would-be fabric. I started to discover a whole world that had gone completely unnoticed until I declared who I was.

As my life started to attract the necessary items to become a full-fledged knitter, I was also continuing through the learning process. I don't remember much about how easy or difficult it was to teach myself the basics. I honestly don't recall if I had a lot of instant success or if I overcame mistake after mistake. But with simple graphics in the "how-to-knit" section of the knitting booklet from Ernie's mom, I taught myself all the basics and I did it all in a self-taught bubble with the only proof of my newfound ability was that I had created a stable fabric with simple yarn and knitting needles.

If you're not a knitter, I can tell you there are extremely strong opinions about the right way of doing certain things in knitting. How to hold and tension the yarn. How to wrap/pick the yarn onto the needle point. Honestly, I'm glad I was able to get to a certain level of basic knitting and even have finished a few projects on my own before I ever showed my efforts to another knitter. I think the disapproval of a real knitter might have made me feel less excited about the newfound identity.

At one point, I decided I had enough tools and knowledge to make a garment in one of the knitting booklets I had borrowed/stolen from Ernie's mom. I decided to make a pair of men's boxer-brief underpants. Yes, I questioned whether wool would be too scratchy for an undergarment. I figured that if they were good enough for the people in the UK in the first half of the 1900's, they were good enough for me. Yes, I also understood that it was an odd choice of projects for an already odd choice in hobbies.

Let me explain. The booklet I stole (let's keep it simple from now on and use the correct verb) was an old booklet from the U.K. called Woolcraft. It was published by a yarn company named Patons and Baldwins. It was the 15th edition of this particular booklet, and while there is no date of publication, most of the descriptions of this booklet indicate it was printed in the 1950's.

The patterns were seemingly from an earlier era and just reprinted in the 1950's perhaps. It contained many vintage items that people used to knit out of necessity. Pram covers, baby bonnets and booties, children's clothes and of course, sweaters, a boy's lumber jacket, socks, underwear, etc.

The photo of the underpants really intrigued me. I loved the thought of having a hand-made pair of underwear, especially with a button-fly and vintage shaping. Given that they were shaped in a similar style to what I was already wearing for commercial underwear, I knew I just had to make them.

Then came the next hurdle – learning how to read a knitting pattern. Reading a knitting pattern is a completely different skill to master than learning knitting itself. It requires understanding gauge, yarn weights, needle sizes, and seemingly hundreds of abbreviations. Even though all the abbreviations had descriptions, they still sometimes seemed quite confusing. For instance, even though SL1 was translated to "slip one stitch", you still had to understand that you moved the next stitch to be worked from the left-hand needle to the right-hand needle without creating a new stitch. But it wasn't clear exactly how to transfer the stitch. There were many similarly unclear directions with no corresponding diagram to help visualize how to do it. I intended to make my best guess and see how it worked.

To add another level of complexity, the booklet was written using UK knitting terms. For instance, the underwear pattern called for two ounces of "Patonised" 3-ply wool, and two number 12 and two number 11 knitting needles. Try going into a yarn store in the U.S. today and asking for these supplies. Most will have no idea what you're talking about. You can imagine how perplexed I was as a new knitter.

In case you're interested in the translation, the term "Patonised" is presumably some proprietary term of Patons and Baldwins for a wool yarn that's been treated in some way. Most probably it would be called superwash wool today. 3-ply wool refers to what most Americans call fingering or sock-weight yarn. Number 12 and number 11 knitting needles are approximately the equivalent of a size 2 and size 2.5 United States knitting needles (2.75 mm diameter and 3 mm diameter needles, respectively).

It is difficult to imagine that so much translation needed to be done between two English-speaking countries.

Despite all of the roadblocks, I was able to purchase the correct kind of yarn and the correct sizes of knitting needles. The pattern called for knitting three flat pieces of fabric - the left side and leg, the right side and leg, and the gusset (the diamond-shaped piece of fabric giving extra room in the crotch).

Starting at the bottom ribbing of the left leg, the pattern started with casting on 118 very small stitches. For a beginner, this seemed like a LOT of stitches to cast on, never mind knit. But it was a good exercise. I soon had the ribbed cuff at the bottom of the left leg finished. I wasn't just creating fabric; I was creating ribbed fabric and it looked really good!

I ended up finishing that first project including following the pattern instructions for knitting buttonholes for the waistband and fly and sewing on buttons.

The underwear looked great and even fit me quite well. I couldn't have been more pleased with my first effort at making a garment.

The amazing discovery I made about knitting this first garment was that knitting is really rather simple. It's not initially very easy, and it takes a lot of perseverance to get good and/or fast at it, but it's not complex. This was an important realization in my early, wobbly steps as I continued to establish an identity. Knitting also didn't really require patience so much as it took perseverance. I quickly realized I had a stubborn amount of perseverance when it came to knitting thousands of individual stitches to complete my first project.

Soon, I realized that as I finished the first project, I would definitely need to try a sweater as my second project. As knitting projects go, a sweater seemed to be the ideal standard for demonstrating my knitting chops. A successful sweater would eliminate any doubt in my mind that I was indeed a knitter. Well, maybe it wouldn't eliminate all doubt.

I'm sure it's quite clear that I had become laser-focused on making knitting a part of my identity. There were a number of reasons to not be a knitter. There were no knitters in my life. There were no men who knit anywhere that I knew of, and there were also no examples of any young people who knit. Despite these reasons, I only became more determined. But the sweater project was going to require that I start interacting with other knitters. Minimally, I was going to have to find someone who could help me choose yarn for the project. It soon became evident that this newfound identity might not survive exposure to an actual knitting community.

While my friend Ernie was able to competently explain how to make a tube of fabric, I didn't know anyone yet who could describe what it was like to create the fabric of community. The invisible pull toward others with a similar excitement about yarn-craft was slower to grow. However, it wasn't any less compelling. The potential for creating community was equally as exciting for me as the possibility of creating fabric with yarn and needles. I just didn't know it yet.

Chapter 2
The Local Yarn Store

"Expectations are resentments waiting to happen."

Anne Lamott

The local yarn store, or LYS as it is commonly referred to in online knitting forums, is the first place many knitters experienced their initial sense of being part of a crafting community. As a new knitter, I had a significant number of ideas and expectations about yarn stores. Many of these ideas weren't even fully formed as complete ideas in my head until they proved to be invalidated by the actual experience of being in a yarn store.

First, I assumed that there wasn't much of a huge demand for yarn. I thought it was most likely there weren't going to be many yarn stores to choose from in my area. This thought was based partly on the assumption that there wasn't a huge number of knitters out there. I anticipated that when a rare knitter came into a local yarn store, their presence would be highly valued to the store. Mostly, my expectations were that I'd be enthusiastically welcomed and helped and encouraged in my efforts. My first visit to a yarn store dispelled those ideas and expectations quickly.

Having decided to make a sweater, I scoured the magazine sections of the local pharmacy and the grocery store for any knitting-related magazines. I finally found what I was looking for. In February of 1988, Woman's Day magazine published their "Super Special 101 Sweater & Craft Ideas" issue. It featured a men's cardigan knit in a Shaker rib stitch pattern. The pattern called for ten skeins of Coats & Clark Red Heart 4 Ply Knit & Crochet yarn in a color called Paddy Green.

Most new knitters choose a project based on the photo of the finished project. They typically want to knit it in the same color as the model wearing it in the magazine or book. Unlike most knitters, I dismissed the idea of green and decided I would find a charcoal-gray yarn to make this sweater.

The closest real yarn store was a small shop in Princeton, New Jersey. Clayton's yarn store was a small boutique in an upscale outdoor shopping area of Princeton called Palmer Square. I thought that I might have to pay a premium price for the yarn I bought at this store based on the location, which, I thought, made it all the more likely that I'd be greeted with enthusiasm.

The minute I entered the store, I felt lost. I had no idea how the store was organized or how to go about finding yarn for my project. Fortunately (or maybe not), the person behind the counter approached me. Looking back on events now, I think she may have been more concerned that I'd touch something in the store that I wasn't supposed to. Instead of coming to help me, I think she may have been more concerned with protecting the store and its contents than in assisting me. But I didn't even consider that at the first moment of interaction. I was still quite excited to be venturing into a new knitting experience.

I showed her the photo of the sweater I wanted to make in the magazine. I proudly told her that it called for 10 skeins of Coats & Clark Red Heart 3-ply yarn. I had memorized that part of the pattern instructions.

If you're a knitter, you can probably imagine the reaction. If you're not, let me just say that Red Heart is a particularly inexpensive acrylic yarn that many natural fiber enthusiasts would be particularly critical of. Suffice it to say this store owner or employee was exactly that kind of enthusiast. She literally turned away from me to go back to her place behind the counter and with obvious disdain said, "We don't carry that yarn."

I seem to remember starting to spin in place looking all around at all the different yarns in the store. At the same time, I was wondering if she meant that this store couldn't help me at all. There were no other customers in the store and I had clearly been dismissed. In a bit of a panic, I asked if they had any yarn that I could use to make the sweater. Her response was as unenthusiastic as it could be: She said dismissively, "We have lots of yarn."

In a matter of seconds, my expectations had gone from being an eager, prized yarn store customer, to someone who needed to grovel and curry favor with the yarn store vendor to get even a little help. I pivoted quickly and offered, "I was hoping to make it in a charcoal gray yarn." Her response was to walk back over near me to a wall of yarn, pick one skein of charcoal gray yarn and hand it to me. With no other information and no idea of what I was buying, I purchased 12 skeins of this charcoal gray yarn. For the curious knitter-reader, it was a wool and cotton blend yarn by Brown Sheep Yarns. Not the ideal yarn for this project, but I'll get to that later.

If you have never been in a yarn store or if you are a yarn store owner or employee, you're probably thinking this was a really bad example of a first-time visit to a yarn store.

If you're a man who's been into a number of yarn stores over the last few decades, you'll probably know that this is an all-too-common experience. You'll also probably understand this feeling of being snubbed in a yarn store if you're a customer that doesn't look like you could afford nice yarn. I'm not sure if the reaction I got was because I was a man, or because I was asking about cheap, acrylic yarn...or some combination of both. I've also heard of yarn stores that just treated all customers with disdain.

Yes, there are many yarn stores that are happy to help anyone that comes through their door. But there are enough of them that also have this elitist, snobby, look-down-their-noses-at-you vibe that is not in the least bit welcoming. I don't pretend to understand it.

Over the years, I came up with a strategy whenever I went into a yarn store for the first time. I would start shopping near a staff member in the store and ask knowledgeable questions about specific yarns. "Is this a superwash wool?" "Do you carry any other sport-weight wool yarn?" "I've always loved Noro yarns' colorways. Your selection of Noro yarns is quite beautiful." I felt the need to establish myself as both an experienced yarn-store customer, but also wanted to ingratiate myself with someone whose help I might need. Even with this tactic, I was often treated with some level of disrespect by people working at yarn stores. I attributed it mostly to the fact that I was a man in a world that they considered to be for women only.

One of my favorite examples of this type of experience was during a visit to a small yarn store in Northern New Jersey. I quickly started my regular routine and engaged the store owner in conversation. I expressed how happy I was that they carried Addi Turbos (a popular brand of knitting needles). I picked up a ball of sock yarn and asked her if any of her customers had had difficulty getting the suggested gauge with this brand of yarn. I even asked if she carried any books on men's knitwear. After all that, I brought my purchases of yarn and needles to the front counter to check out and as she rang up my items, she said, "Are you buying all of this for your wife?" Even as a witty gay man, I was left speechless.

Things have largely changed with yarn stores over the last 40 years. In my early days of knitting, it used to be that about one out of every three stores I'd visit were unfriendly or sometimes even hostile. These days it's a lot rarer to experience that kind of response. The visibility of men in fiber crafts has grown with representation in social media and online forums, so staff at yarn stores are less surprised by the presence of someone like me. Also, with so many online vendors where one can purchase yarn and tools, customer service can differentiate a yarn store and give them some advantage in the marketplace. There is still some disdain for people looking for cheap, acrylic yarns. There is also some lack of patience for newer knitters who are unsure of what they're looking for. But in general, most yarn stores I go to understand how to value their customers and make them feel welcome.

There were a number of reasons that I never went back to Clayton's in Princeton (it's been long out of business, so that you don't think I have a hidden agenda here). You'll read shortly that I did use the yarn I purchased there to knit my first sweater, and it wasn't an ideal choice in yarns. I really did resent the woman who treated me so gruffly and sold less-than-ideal yarn to an unsuspecting new knitter. But mainly, my lack of patronage was because I found another yarn store - one that encouraged me. This yarn store tried to make as many new knitters into obsessive knitters as they could. Shortly after the experience in the Princeton yarn store, I moved to a town in Pennsylvania that was only a couple of miles away from a nationally known yarn store. That yarn store truly started me on my journey of seeking out and communing with like-minded people.

Despite my first unpleasant yarn store experience, I did go on to knit my first sweater. It wasn't great, but it was good enough to level up to a stage where I could officially identify as a knitter.

Chapter 3
The Arctic Sweater

"I am always doing that which I cannot do, in order that I may learn how to do it."

Pablo Picasso

Taking on a full sweater project presented some challenges. The pattern called for knitting a fisherman's rib fabric, which required that I learn a new stitch pattern. I found it awkward to execute this particular stitch pattern. The combination of having a tight tensioning with my knitting and having to knit two stitches together made my hands ache after a while. Part of the difficulty was also due to the cotton component of the yarn. Cotton yarn has very little elasticity compared to wool and so inserting the tip of the knitting needle into a tight, non-elastic stitch proved to be physically difficult.

As with the underpants, this sweater was knit in sections. Two front sections, the back, two sleeves and a button band were all knit separately. This required that the individual sections be sewn together. And each of the seams were joining different edges of the knitted fabric together. Knitting patterns don't tell you how to attach knitted fabric together, so I was on my own in trying to figure out how to secure all these pieces together with their varying edge-joins.

The final result of my fledgling sweater project was a perfectly acceptable first attempt at a cardigan for a new knitter. But like many knitters, all I could see were the bad choices and mistakes in the garment. I've found this interesting quirk about many crafters. They're often very willing to point out every mistake in a completed project. I definitely have this quirk too. I'm not normally a perfectionist, especially with a new venture. But there were a number of aspects of the making of this sweater that I wished I had done differently.

First of all, the finished cardigan was very heavy. Fisherman's rib fabric is a thick and dense fabric. Since it was made with yarn that was pretty heavy to begin with, it made a garment that Thaddeus dubbed, "the Arctic sweater" because it could keep you warm even in the Arctic. Secondly, I wasn't overly satisfied with the various seams where I had sewn the pieces together. They were both bulky and sometimes not very neat looking. Finally, I had to figure out a better way of executing a very common instruction in knit patterns, "Bind off loosely."

One benefit to a densely knit fabric is that it's very durable. I still have the sweater and I even wear it once in a while. To be honest, I like it. But if I were to offer my younger self some helpful criticism, here's what I'd say:

> *On a positive note, the sweater is well-fitting and looks great on you. In addition to taking on a new stitch technique of fisherman's rib, you knit a sweater with pockets and a sewn-on neckband. All impressive for a first-time sweater.*
>
> *The first area of noticeable improvements you could have made was in the binding off. The most obvious example of that is how tight the top of your pocket*

> *edging is. It should be looser. Also, the finishing techniques on your garment need work. Sewing together the seam at the top of the shoulders and where the sleeve attaches to the armhole both should be done differently and with more care and patience.*
>
> *Finally, your choice in yarn fiber content was really bad for this garment. You chose a cotton and wool blend yarn that is way too heavy and dense for this stitch pattern, and as a result, your sweater weighs a ton and is probably impenetrable by bullets. You may have accidentally invented knitted Kevlar.*

Okay, perhaps those last few critiques were a little less than helpful, but it was a very dense and heavy garment.

There were some other things that were a bit random about the sweater, one of which you'll have to wait until the next chapter to find out about. But many of the issues with my sweater knitting were associated with impatience and reluctance to go back and undo something that could have been done better. The buttons, for instance, were from an old rugby shirt that I had outgrown. Instead of figuring out the best place to buy appropriate buttons, I recycled some from an old shirt. Not such an awful thing, except that rugby shirts use rubber buttons (to avoid injuries, I'm assuming). Rubber buttons aren't exactly ideal for a wool and cotton cardigan.

All in all, still not bad for a first sweater. All of the difficulties and complexities were opportunities for learning and vowing that next time I'd do it better. Because I definitely looked forward to a next time.

As for the really bad choice in yarn? I could blame Clayton's yarn store for years about that. Perhaps.

Chapter 4
Another Man Who Knits

"My conviction gains infinitely the moment another soul will believe in it."

E.M. Forster

While it was Ernie who introduced me to knitting, and I had met a few dozen other knitters, I hadn't yet met any other guy who had taken up knitting. I was often reminded that some famous football player from the fifties and sixties was a knitter. Yes, despite my distaste of sports, I was familiar with Rosey Grier (one of the 'fearsome foursome') who was best known as a "real guy" who did needlepoint. Though he did also knit and crochet as well, from what I understand. It did not go unnoticed how often people would try to normalize my non-gender-conforming hobby by referring to Rosey Grier. The other piece of trivia that is often mentioned is that knitting was originally done exclusively by men. The knitting guilds in Europe are mentioned where knitting was a valued skill that required years of apprenticing and training to be able to be a member of the guild - until it was automated, and only then was hand-knitting relegated to women as busy work.

If people had really noticed how perfectly excited I was to have found knitting as a hobby, they might have realized how unnecessary it was to try and make me feel comfortable with my choice in hobbies. I'm assuming these justifications were more to ease their own discomfort than to encourage me.

As chance would have it, I had met a friend through a local social group. Bob was also a gay man in a relationship. He and his partner Alan had moved to the area recently and purchased an old mill that had been converted into a residence. They were looking to expand their social circle. Having yet to meet each other's partners, I invited Bob and Alan to our house for dinner. Pre-dinner chatting somehow came to the topic of knitting.

Now I know the hardcore knitters are rolling their eyes over the word "somehow" in that last sentence. They know that any get-together that includes at least one knitter will always have the topic of knitting come up in conversation. It's like the old joke, "How do you know someone is a knitter? Trust me, they'll tell you!" It seems as though fanatical people are always prone to discussing their fanaticism. But I was just a budding fanatic. So it was still just a happy coincidence that the topic of knitting was brought up. Really.

Happy, because it turns out that Alan is a knitter. He's not only a knitter, but he's an incredibly experienced and talented knitter who worked with clothing companies to design various knitted fabric patterns for mass-production of sweaters in various clothing lines. But before we learned all of his background, when we found out that he knit, Thaddeus very supportively mentioned that I was a knitter and I had knit both underwear and a sweater. He urged me to go upstairs and bring down the two items I had knit and show them to Alan.

In addition to being excited, I was actually a bit nervous and bashful. It was the first time anyone other than Thaddeus had ever seen my sweater and now a real knitter was about to see it. Thankfully, Alan was supportive and encouraging. Honestly, I would have been too, in the same situation. My first two knitted garments were relatively advanced for someone just learning. I think Alan was expecting to see something a lot more rudimentary for my first two projects…like a lumpy scarf in cheap acrylic yarn (which I also think is impressive, and also a little more expected from a new knitter).

After appraising my work in a very positive way, he also told me in a supportive way that I was knitting incorrectly. He told me that my stitches were twisted. I had no idea what he meant. I had clearly been successful in creating a stable fabric with uniform stitches that had been formed into wearable garments. He pointed to the underwear to show me how the fabric that should be relatively flat was a little less flat than it should be. So Alan gave me my first in-person lesson in knitting.

He asked me to show him how I knit, so I demonstrated. He didn't see anything wrong with it. Then he asked me to show him how I purled, so I did. He realized immediately that I was wrapping the yarn around the needle in the wrong direction (for non-knitters–you typically wrap the yarn around the needle in a counterclockwise direction). The result was that I was twisting each stitch. Normally, I might bristle at a critique in other areas of my life, but when it came to knitting, I was very excited to receive feedback. With no other resources than a knitting booklet, I was like a desert getting a brief rain shower and wanting to soak in every drop.

It was almost as exciting as Ernie's first description of creating knitted tubular fabric. I was so thrilled that someone who actually knew how to knit could show me how to do it correctly. He said something odd after he showed me how to purl correctly. He said, "You're probably not going to ever change because you're used to the way you're doing it." Which couldn't have been more inaccurate. I assured him that I was planning on changing the way I purled immediately and I would always do it correctly from then on. It was as though he had passed on the rites of passage into a mysterious society or the secret handshake is probably more accurate. I had become a bona fide member.

The other thing about learning the correct way to purl is that it explains so much about issues I was having with my knitting.

First off, twisted stitches make it difficult to insert the needle to make a stitch. It's difficult to describe in written text, but basically when a loop of yarn sits on the needle in the proper position, it's quite easy to insert the point of the other needle into that loop to execute a new stitch. But when that loop sits on the needle in a twisted position, it can feel very awkward to insert the point of the other needle into it. Like many new knitters, I was a tight knitter to begin with, so it was even more difficult to physically make a knit stitch based on how I taught myself to purl.

Second, twisting stitches creates a very dense and stiff fabric. If you can imagine a nice, loose and drapey fabric made up of thousands of yarn-loops. Then imagine adding a twist to each of those thousands of loops, then you might be able to understand how dense and heavy it would make the resulting fabric. No wonder my first sweater fabric was so thick! A poor choice in yarn that was too heavy and dense, combined with a technique that made the resulting fabric even more dense, and–voilà! We have the Arctic sweater.

It wasn't all the fault of the impatient store-clerk's poor selection of yarn after all. But lest we forget, she was still a rather awful person to staff a yarn store for other reasons too!

There were many amazing results of this first-time meeting of another knitter. I was able to learn how to knit (or purl) correctly. But it was also one of those moments in time where I got to realize that I wasn't alone. Alan encouraged and supported me in continuing to knit. He even chastised me for critiquing my own efforts, insisting that my efforts were quite impressive. He modeled for me what would eventually become my way of encouraging other new knitters that I would soon meet.

Learning to be encouraging and enthusiastic about someone else's knitting was also my first lesson in creating the fabric of community. A supportive environment, especially for new knitters, would be an important component of establishing a stable community going forward.

This interaction was probably the pivotal event that I needed to take on the identity of a knitter without any hesitation. I just needed a little bit of validation that my choice in hobbies could be seen as acceptable. It also gave me the thirst to meet, interact with, and learn from other knitters. As my knitting community started to coalesce, Alan didn't seem to have any desire to participate. He either didn't seem to have any gravitational pull toward surrounding himself with like-minded people, or he relished his outsider status so much that an affirming community might ruin his rebel-reputation. Over the years, I was grateful for Alan's continued guidance in his areas of expertise, and the early push he gave me toward becoming a more self-assured knitter.

Chapter 5
The Local Yarn Store – Take Two!

"The truth is: Belonging starts with self-acceptance. Your level of belonging, in fact, can never be greater than your level of self-acceptance, because believing that you're enough is what gives you the courage to be authentic, vulnerable and imperfect."

Brené Brown

The Tomato Factory

There was a yarn store called the Tomato Factory in Lambertville, New Jersey. It started out as both a combined yarn wholesaler and retailer housed in a former tomato canning factory in a neighboring town. They were the business that brought some brilliant European knitwear designers to the attention of knitters in this country. The store was considered a high-end yarn store, in that it carried high-quality yarn brands. They sold both mail-order (via the phone, since there were very few internet yarn sales yet) and directly out of their funky storefront in a great little river town. Lambertville is one of the many towns up and down the Delaware River that separates New Jersey from Pennsylvania along most of their shared border.

The yarn store was in an old firehouse. It was owned and staffed by incredibly creative and talented fiber artists. My initial experience was a bit worrying, but my worries were short-lived.

As usual, upon entering, I began chatting up the staff. There was an incredibly chic and stylish woman staffing the store that first day I went. She was easygoing and friendly and as I tried to prove my knitting bona fides with intelligent comments about yarn and knitting, she chatted about new yarns they had just gotten in. This store had also knit up small swatches of fabric in many of the yarns on their shelf so I could see how the yarn looked when knit into fabric. One of the swatches fascinated me. It was a very stretchy, thin terry-cloth-like fabric. I told the salesperson how much I like it. She said, "Yes, that's Adrienne Vittadini!" She said it as if I (and everyone else) knew the name. I mumbled something about not being familiar, and she insisted, "Of course you know who Adrienne Vittadini is!" I assured her I didn't and she responded with a dismissive wave of her hand and insisted again, "Of course you do!"

In my mind, we agreed to disagree.

Despite this first awkward interaction, Carol and I soon became friends. She had an amazing eye for color and design. But more importantly for me, she enthusiastically encouraged me to try anything and everything when it came to knitting. If I saw a brilliant, multi-colored yarn on their shelves, she would suggest ideas for putting it to good use. If I needed suggestions for a baby gift, she didn't limit my imagination to a pastel, yellow blanket. Not once did she ever indicate that some technique or idea was beyond my capabilities. So, it never seemed daunting to take on an advanced project. In fact, it never occurred to me that some people would think that a knitting project was beyond their capabilities. As I noted earlier, knitting is rather simple. It can take a long time and the instructions might be confusing, but usually the actual knitting is quite simple. Plus, I already had a lot of confidence in my ability to learn something that might be difficult. Carol just always encouraged my growth, both creatively and technically. Perhaps my fearless approach to knitting was based on ignorance, but even as I grew less ignorant of all that went into knitting, I never felt like anything was less than exciting to learn.

I started meeting other customers at my local yarn store. The Tomato Factory would host various knit-related events. I remember meeting a number of other customers when I took a workshop on mitered knitting led by the author of a new book on the subject. There was also the time I got to join the staff and customers at a book signing for a famous knitwear designer. On an even larger scale, the store participated in an annual convention called Stitches, so I'd go and learn about other yarn stores as well. I could find out about new and interesting yarns and knitting techniques. There was a large marketplace at Stitches where yarn vendors had booths and sold yarn, tools, patterns, kits and anything fiber-related you could imagine.

This first positive experience with a yarn store turned out to be my introduction to a new and budding community of knitters.

I started to become known as "the guy who knits" among the knitting community at the yarn store and also among my friends and family. People inevitably started to ask me to knit them things. I grew very good at telling people that I wouldn't knit them a sweater, or an afghan or a baby blanket. Mostly because the non-knitters who asked, really had no idea how much went into a knitted garment. Nor did they understand how much good yarn costs. Actually, I came up with a pat answer to any requests for hand knits, "I'll put you on the list." It was my polite way of saying, "Don't hold your breath."

One instance of being asked to knit something came from a friend who lived in Lambertville. He both knew that I was a knitter and that I shopped for knitting supplies at Tomato Factory. He purchased a multi-part birthday gift for me of a yarn swift, a ball-winder and a gift certificate at Tomato Factory for $200. A swift is a great little spinning gizmo that manages a skein of yarn while you wind it into a ball or cake. You know those times you've seen a cartoon of some dutiful husband holding his spouse's yarn while it gets wound into a ball? That husband's job is eliminated with a yarn swift.

My friend's gift was incredibly thoughtful and generous. But I think he also knew me well enough that I would have to come up with something equally as thoughtful and generous for his next birthday. Turns out that he mentioned to the staff at The Tomato Factory that he loved the sweater in one of the kits at their store. The kit cost just under $200! I think perhaps I had been set up.

Fortunately, the kit was a challenging looking project by an amazing artist and knitwear designer named Kaffe Fassett (to assist you in the pronunciation, he will tell you that his name rhymes with "safe asset"). It was a shawl-collared cardigan designed in spectacular colors, called Ancient Jacket. It used over 25 colors of yarn in a knitted color-work technique called intarsia, where different sections of each row are worked in different colors to create sections of color. It was a new technique for me and I was always excited to learn something new. But it was even more complicated in that the directions for the sections of color were in a gridded chart form. Each pixel of the grid was a stitch in a particular color of yarn. If that wasn't complex enough, the color of each stitch was made up of one, two or three strands of the 25 different colors of yarn.

I describe the complexity of the design not to tell you how intimidated I was, but to make it clear how intimidated I wasn't. Carol at the yarn store had done a good job of normalizing the simplicity of just knitting one stitch at a time. She gave me some vague instructions about how to do intarsia knitting and I couldn't wait to get started.

With my new ball-winder and swift, I quickly wound all the yarn for the project into center-pull balls of yarn and cast on with excitement.

It was a complete success and the result was truly impressive. Kaffe's design was sublime and the yarn was incredibly rich and beautiful. Simply following straightforward instructions, I had been able to create an amazing garment. With resources at the Tomato Factory who could show me how to bind off loosely and how to best sew the separate pieces together, the sweater came out practically perfect. My friend received it as a birthday gift. While I don't think he was surprised at the content of the gift, I think he was surprised at how well it came out and he looked fantastic in it.

As I continued to involve myself with my local yarn store, they eventually asked me if I wanted to work there a few hours on Sundays. For the last few years that they were in business, I worked Sunday afternoons, but it wasn't work for me. It was joyous and fun to be around other knitters. I loved helping people with yarn purchases, color selections, project ideas and mostly encouraging them with as much enthusiasm as I had been shown by the staff at the store. I would often tell people that I worked at Tomato Factory for the discount, but truth be told, my desire to be around like-minded enthusiasts was the real reason. My involvement in the knitting community paralleled the multi-color design of Kaffe's intarsia sweater by joining my joy, enthusiasm and newfound skills in unexpected ways with the existing vibrancy of the customers at The Tomato Factory to create a feeling of belonging that was exhilarating and beautiful.

It was in this supportive and encouraging community that I began to design knitwear. My first design idea was meant to help the store sell more of a specific yarn. I designed a scarf to make use of a vibrantly beautiful, multi-color, fine-gauge yarn. The yarn was described as hand-painted and was dyed in a variety of unexpected and interesting color combinations. While the yarn vendor published a number of knitting patterns using their own yarn, most of them didn't show off the beauty of the yarn as well as I thought they could. I looked for a stitch pattern to make a scarf that blended the colors in ways that would highlight the vibrant colorways of the yarns without creating an overall muddy mix of colors. I didn't anticipate that the scarf design would be written up as a pattern, since I had simply taken a well-known stitch pattern, called Feather and Fan and combined it with two different colorways of the multi-color yarn. But with a couple of examples of this new scarf hanging in the store, customers asked to know how to make it. So I wrote up my first knitting pattern.

Documenting a design made me realize how much goes into directions for a knitting pattern. Remember those seemingly hundreds of abbreviations I had to learn about when I first started using patterns to knit? My first knitting pattern needed some of those abbreviations. But it also required dimensions of the finished product, needle sizes used, yardage of yarn needed and the number of stitches-per-inch that should be created to get the proper gauge. All that for a simple, rectangular-shaped piece of knitted fabric. It gave me an incredible appreciation for all the knitting patterns I had used up until that point, especially for shapes more complex than a long rectangle.

The next phase in my design career came when I modified a design by one of the yarn store's staff. She had created a women's horizontal-striped cardigan in four different, rich colors. I thought they'd make a perfect men's pullover, so I created that garment for myself. Again, customers wanted the pattern, so I wrote it up.

Taking well-known stitch patterns or modifying someone else's design to create something new was like using training wheels while learning to ride a bike. My third design continued to rely on training wheels. I was shopping for clothes in an Abercrombie & Fitch store and they had a simple v-neck pullover for sale that I really liked. It was a solid color with two contrasting color stripes across the chest - very collegiate looking. It occurred to me that I could easily recreate this design with a hand-knit. So I did. I began to get better at documenting everything about the knitting process so that I could more easily write up a pattern for the design once the garment was complete.

The Tomato Factory decided to close its doors sometime in the '90's. Fortunately, Carol and a few of the employees at the store decided to open a new yarn store in the same town. The new store was called Simply Knit and the owners were very talented knit and crochet designers. While my designing was still pretty basic, I still felt a part of the new store by creating designs that would help them sell yarn. I was able to help them out in the newly emerging technical arena by managing their mailing list (postal mail, not email) and eventually setting up a website for them so that they could have a presence on the newfangled world-wide web. I found that I had already woven my unique set of skills into the local knitting community in a way that made the fabric of this community better.

Establishing myself as part of this local yarn store community was the most important introduction I had to the larger knitting community. Many knitters found a welcoming and encouraging community at similar local yarn shops around the world. We'd gather to talk about a great new yarn we'd discovered, or show off the latest sweater design we were working on. The local yarn store was where many of us started to feel a sense of belonging.

It also turned out to be an invaluable on-ramp to the budding online knitting community.

Chapter 6
The Digital Age of Community

"I know there is strength in the differences between us. I know there is comfort, where we overlap."

Ani DiFranco

At the point when I started becoming interested in the internet, I had spent a bit over a decade becoming a knitter. While I had established myself in small, local communities like my local yarn store group, it still seemed like a temporary assignment until I found my true place in the knitting world.

It was in the early part of the 1990s and we were starting to hear more and more about the internet. There weren't many options for accessing this mysterious world-wide web. At least there weren't many options for accessing it that didn't require a lot of technical skills - skills I didn't have. However, my work was beginning to be more computer-based, so I was quickly gaining an understanding of technology.

In 1986, I took a job with a Wall Street-based insurance company. I became the person responsible for their employee database. The information was entered onto a mainframe computer in Roanoke, Virginia and I could access it through "dead terminals" in the downtown New York City office. These terminals were screens that would only connect to our mainframe and send and receive commands via the associated keyboard. They were referred to as dead terminals because, disconnected from the mainframe they had no ability to process anything on their own. We only had two of these terminals in our work area. One was on a desk near mine and the other was in a back room used for file storage and shredding documents. A longtime employee, Trisha, in my department was responsible for updating some of the employee benefits information on our system, but she also ran a process that encrypted the data every night to protect the security of the employees' information. The following morning, we would un-encrypt the data so we could use it in our daily work.

Trisha was in the middle of running the encryption routine one night on the back-room terminal when the system went down. In all likelihood, we just lost the connection to the mainframe, but since she was concerned the data hadn't been fully encrypted, she decided that all would be fine if she just locked the door to the back room to secure access to the terminal she had used to run the encryption routine.

Understanding that there was no physical data on that terminal, and locking the door would do nothing to secure private data, I understood how some people viewed computers, connectivity and data storage. Her misunderstanding of technology provided me with some valuable insight. I was starting to gain a basic understanding of technology, and the interconnectivity of systems.

During this time, many of us had decided to bring ourselves into the future with a personal computer at home. Companies like Gateway and their familiar cow-spotted boxes were showing up more and more. I had familiarity with computers from work and I had decided to purchase a home computer in case I wanted to do some work without having to be in the office. My work at the time included accessing the mainframe computer through a PC-based interface program. For a number of years, I had a specialized board installed in my desktop computer at work which allowed me to make my PC simulate a mainframe dead terminal. Setting up a similar hardware on my home computer allowed me to do some limited work from home. Mostly, it was used for responding to urgent requests. But more importantly, it gave me a feel for the potential for interconnectivity between computers. My computer wasn't an isolated, stand-alone machine any longer. It was connected to another much larger computer.

That interconnectivity quickly expanded with the internet. Back then, America Online (AOL) used to send out CDs in the mail. I seem to recall receiving a lot of these discs. AOL had found a way of making it simple to access the internet from a home computer. I loaded an AOL disc on my computer and signed up for their monthly dial-up service. The initial registration for AOL required that I choose a screen name. Since the internet was still a bit of a mystery to me, I wasn't sure how public I wanted to be in this new world, but I wanted a screen name that was both descriptive and that would allow me to maintain privacy if I needed to.

This was right around the time I started reading about how the LGBT community was starting to reclaim the word queer as a term of pride rather than derision. The screen name "QueerJoe" seemed like the perfect way to go. It was just in-your-face enough and prideful enough to express exactly how I wanted to be seen online. Just the presence of my new screen name in an AOL chat room could cause a bit of an uproar. So, I quickly grew comfortable with the anonymity that my new AOL screen name afforded me.

I gained an understanding of how my world and the virtual world could cross over. AOL had web browsing, email, chat rooms and AOL Messenger for messaging. This rapid expansion of access to people and information was both daunting and exciting for me. I quickly understood that I was jumping into a much bigger community of the world with a simple click of a mouse.

While the lines between my work world and technology were blurring with this new technology, so were the lines between my identity as a knitter and the rest of the knitting world.

One of the least technically-oriented employees at the Simply Knit yarn store had heard a rumor about something called the KnitList and she suggested it was something I might want to investigate. Someone had written down some basic words that could be used to find this new group, so I checked it out. It turns out that the KnitList was an online group of knitters who had subscribed to a listserv.

A listserv was basically an internet/email application that allowed users to subscribe and communicate via group emails. Listservs were being set up to create specific affinity groups for a vast number of different topics, including knitting. Once I became a member, any emails sent to the listserv would be echoed out to all the members of that group, either as individual emails or as one daily consolidated email "digest" with all the emails that came in on a particular day.

The rudimentary new method of corresponding with other knitters around the world was revolutionary at the time. Nothing like it had ever existed and it clearly satisfied a desire we didn't even know we had - of bringing together large numbers of knitters. When I first joined, the KnitList was run by a knitter named Emily Way and was hosted on a web server at the University of Michigan. The KnitList facilitated discussions, requests for knitting help, patterns and a vast and varied archive of links and helpful resources for knitters. The KnitList was considered quite active. By 1999 they had over 2200 members worldwide, and averaged 90 messages per day. That may seem small in comparison to the size of online communities today, but it was a massive increase from the pre-internet days.

Like any community, it attracted members at all levels of knitting skills. It was on the KnitList that I began to see where I fit in this ever-growing world of knitters. It also allowed me to establish relationships with people, some of whom I'm still friends with over a quarter of a century later. As happens in many communities, we formed small cliques of people with whom we shared commonalities and interests.

The fabric of my community began to take shape in these smaller cliques. I found I had little patience for certain personality traits. Hesitant, unsure knitters who had to canvas the entire population of the KnitList before they knit a test-swatch, were probably the people who were the least like me. They were not at all what I aspired to be. I also struggled with people who desperately wanted to take part in the community, but did so in seemingly lazy, thoughtless ways. They would send one-word responses to a long string of emails, like "Congrats!" when someone had finished a project. It didn't seem necessary or useful to me. It annoyed me (probably way more than it should have) when members wasted my time with posts that didn't seem to forward or add to the conversation. I was also quite wary of people who posted with a clear political, religious and/or marketing agenda.

One rule of the list was to exclude controversial issues from one's posts. It was impossible to censor out controversy completely, so some members would find ways around it. Flame wars would erupt. Every year, around the December holidays, there was always a round of contentious posts to the KnitList that became known as the "War on Christmas". An atheist or non-religious member would take offense when someone would wish everyone a Merry Christmas and some Christians would take offense when people would wish everyone a "Happy Holiday" or something that left the "Christ out of Christmas." It was always amazing to me how petty and mean people would get around December each year. It was also quite tiresome when it became a regular, annual thing.

The person who annoyed me the most by far was a woman who had an automatic signature file at the end of all of her emails that read, "Blessings to all, whether you think you need them or not." The hubris of her forced blessing, combined with my own feelings of being damaged by religion in my youth, made this seem completely antithetical to fostering a vibrant, supportive community. Her signature-statement sent the message that she considered me (and others like me) to be less-than and in need of repair via her blessings. It angered me every time I read it. If listservs could allow you to block someone, I would have blocked this one person. But the valuable part of this member's tagline was that it allowed me to see there was an organic direction and purpose to the KnitList, which was to foster and encourage community. This member's post made the purpose all the more obvious by how it went against that general direction. Sometimes witnessing what doesn't work in a group, highlights what does work even more vibrantly.

It was rare that my response to a person on the KnitList was as strong as it was for this person. But whether it was a strong reaction to someone, or just a general disinterest in a member's posts, I began to use these evaluations to design a fabric of community that I wanted in my life. Most of the members of the KnitList shared my passion for yarn and fiber-work, but I realized that there were additional characteristics that I desired in my group of like-minded folks. I continued to filter out those with whom I did not feel I shared values, and that left me with those who felt like "my people."

I started to favor snarky, cynical people who had a bit of sarcasm to their posts. I was also drawn to the supportive and knowledgeable folks on the list and I had great appreciation for the astute newbies to the list who took the time to "read the room" and post in a way that was consistent with the purpose of the KnitList. At one point, a searchable archive of the KnitList became available. The KnitList had a Frequently Asked Questions (FAQ) section that responded to the queries that were too often repeated from newbies who didn't take the time to research before posting. The administrators of the group even included a tired, knit-related joke, noting that it had been posted numerous times, and was no longer humorous or welcomed. The joke was about a woman speeding down the highway while knitting and a policeman pulling up beside her yelling "Pull over!", to which she replies, "No, cardigan!" For you non-knitters out there, just know that most jokes that are knitting-related have been heard by knitters a number of times by the time you will have come across it.

One other true gift of the KnitList is that I began to see other men on this knitting forum. There were not many of them, but the posts from guys on this forum always got more attention from me. While I might skim through most of the posts in the daily digest of emails, I would read every word if it was from another male knitter. Like a gravitational pull, I wanted to engage with these rare and kindred members of the KnitList.

The KnitList and listservs in general were very basic means of connecting with groups of people. You could only send text and basic emoticons, such as :-) with no images or file attachments. But even this bare-bones method of communicating with others was a huge leap forward. The one thing you could include in an email to the KnitList was a link to a URL. That's where I started to see that there was a way to share photos and other media on the KnitList via the use of blogs.

Over the years, listservs were replaced with more user-friendly platforms, such as Yahoo Groups and even more recently with forums on various social media platforms. The number of virtually-connected knitters has grown substantially since the simple beginnings of the KnitList. The newer platforms have also allowed us to form smaller, more personalized and specific groups–Northeast Gay Sock Knitters, Australian Bears Who Knit, and so forth.

But the place that brought many of us together in our first large-scale community was the KnitList.

Chapter 7
Knit Blogging

"The man never had a thought that went un-uttered."

Jere B.

Imagine or remember a world before social media, where expressing yourself was primarily done as part of in-person, group settings. If you were curious about someone, you would need to establish some level of relationship with them to be able to find out more about them. Rudimentary groups like the KnitList allowed for broader access to others with whom you might want to get to know. And I seemed to have an innate desire to search out others that I wanted to include in my expanding world.

Two KnitList members in particular began to stand out to me – Marilyn Roberts and Wendy Johnson. Both of them had begun writing blogs about their knitting and posting links to their blog entries to the KnitList whenever they'd publish a new blog entry. I checked their blogs every day so I could read about not just their knitting, but their day-to-day lives as well.

The WendyKnits blog was an ongoing text and photo documentary of Wendy's knitting projects. She is a talented and prolific knitter. Hers was one of the customer names I knew from the two yarn stores where I had worked. She created some of the most beautiful Fair Isle sweaters. Many of them were designed by a well-known knitwear designer that Tomato Factory had helped make famous here in the

United States. Wendy had a throng of fervent followers of her blog.

Marilyn wrote under the name, The Knitting Curmudgeon. She was based relatively close by, out of New Jersey, and she was also a very talented knitter. We eventually became close friends. She wasn't so much a curmudgeon as she was a snarky, sharp and wickedly funny person. You could definitely say that she did not suffer fools gladly. Her controversial blog entries garnered a lot of attention, both positive and negative.

Reading the blogs of these two women, I knew I had to start writing a blog of my own. This was a new way of expressing myself that I was strongly drawn towards. Mostly it was ego-based, in that I wanted to see if I could garner interest like Wendy and Marilyn had. But I had also been looking for some way of documenting my knitting and yarn purchases, organizing my projects, indexing knitting tools and notions and expressing my design ideas. I figured a blog would be the best way of accomplishing all of that.

Blog is short for weblog. It was a new idea back then and it was an arena in which you could participate only if you had some level of technical skills. To be able to publish a blog, you needed to be able to both write and publish HTML code. An understanding of File Transfer Protocol (FTP) was necessary to be able to post blog entries and images to the web. You also had to be able to get decent digitized photos. In those days, most people were still getting photographs developed at Fotomat booths. You also had to understand where you could store your blog entries so that they could be accessed anywhere on this newfangled world-wide web.

I think I had the very minimum skills and equipment necessary to create a blog of my own.

Thankfully, I found an early shortcut regarding publishing a blog. I quickly learned that I didn't have to create HTML code from scratch. I could find a web page I wanted to copy and view the "source". Being able to copy the code that someone else had already created made my first efforts at blogging much easier. It gave me a basic template where I could just change the date, title, headings, text and any images.

I also had a digital camera that I had purchased in Hong Kong when I was there on business. It was a Sony Mavica that literally required that you insert a floppy disk into the back of it to store your images, so I had the means to capture digital imagery and transfer it to my computer and then to a web server. I wasn't completely sure I could get it posted to a blog entry. I wasn't sure I knew all the ins and outs of transferring a digital image to a web server and then having my blog HTML code display the stored photo. Just knowing it could be done, I was certain that I'd figure it out, so I plunged right in.

When setting up the new blog, I decided to use my AOL identity and claimed my own URL or domain name, queerjoe.com, from Network Solutions. They were really the only place that was registering domain names back then. They also allowed me to purchase space on their web servers where I could store my HTML and digital images to make them publicly visible on the internet.

On November 11, 2002, I posted my first blog entry.

> **Monday, November 11, 2002**
>
> **Welcome to the first entry in my personal knitting blog!**
>
> *First, a little about me. I'm a 43 year old gay man, and I've been in a relationship with my partner for 19 years (as of Friday of this week).*
>
> *I've been knitting for about 18 years, and it is my primary passion in life. I learned to knit by reading a basic pattern book from the early 1900's from Paton's. As such, I taught myself to make men's underwear as one of my first projects. They were made in fine baby-weight merino wool, and looked a lot like the boxer-briefs that you can buy today. Going back to my roots, I just purchased some off-white baby-weight merino to make myself underwear again.*
>
> *I've knit sweaters, socks, blankets, felted purses and slippers, toys, afghans, hats and gloves. I make a lot of gifts, and I also knit a lot for my partner and myself. I always have multiple projects being worked on. Right now, I'm actively working on a sweater kit from Scotland for my partner's sister (I call her my sister-out-of-law). She bought the kit expecting to knit it herself, but never got to it. I finally convinced her to bring it to me so she could at least have the sweater as a remembrance of her trip to Scotland (instead of a bag of wool).*
>
> *I've also got a Koigu kit for an Oriental Jacket that's ¼ finished, an afghan experiment to replicate something my partner's grandmother made for him, and a few other projects that I wouldn't exactly say were being actively worked on.*
>
> *I do some designing for a local yarn store near my home, so you can see additional pictures of me modeling some of my work if you go to http://www.simplyknit.com/.*
>
> *I'll eventually be putting pictures of my handiwork out here as I work on it so you can get a sense about how much I actually knit.*
>
> Posted by Joe Wilcox at 4:21 PM 0 comments

It may not seem like much, especially since there are many applications on the internet today where you can easily publish a blog including photos and even videos for no cost and for very little effort and digital cameras are now carried around in our pockets. But back then, I would type up the HTML in a text file and transfer it to the web server folder via FTP. It all seemed like magic in those days and it was exhilarating. Being unsure if I was going to be able to display images on my blog, I decided to try my first image posting. Two weeks after my first blog post, I successfully posted a photo of a sweater I had made for Thaddeus' sister. It was another feat of magic, and I began to start trusting my ability to navigate the new technology. In the first blog entry, Thaddeus's sister was dubbed the "sister-out-of-law" since Thaddeus and I weren't allowed to legally marry for many years after those first few blog entries. My blog soon became both about knitting and about LGBTQ issues.

With the ability to blog, I now had to decide on exactly what kind of blog I wanted to write. Did I want to be like

WendyKnits or like The Knitting Curmudgeon or something altogether different?

The characteristics I liked about Wendy's blog were that she posted regularly and had a significant amount of knitting content. Her knitting was truly impressive. I had gotten very proficient and even prolific in my knitting, but I still couldn't generate an adult-sized Fair Isle sweater in a week like Wendy seemed to be able to do. Wendy also consistently posted entries to her blog. Her many blog readers became accustomed to reading her blog on a relatively frequent and regular basis. Finally, she also did blog contests and giveaways to encourage reader participation. Her readers were very engaged and very loyal to her.

What I didn't like about Wendy's blog is that her writing was less vibrant than I preferred, as were the comments from her readership. Her words seemed very impersonal and flat and they definitely didn't match the beauty of her knitted projects. And her readership seemed only slightly engaged in Wendy's life and put little effort in participating in the blog. Each time she'd post a newly finished, spectacularly beautiful sweater, she'd get dozens of one-word comments. "Beautiful!" "Stunning!" "Gorgeous!" "Amazing!" Again, I was irritated with people who wanted to exert the least amount of energy to be a participant in Wendy's blog community.

Marilyn relied on igniting controversy and sometimes outrage with her readers. She became the Dorothy Parker of knit-bloggers. In fact, Marilyn called her blog readers "tonstant weaders" referring to a famous reaction to a

Winnie-the-Pooh book that Dorothy Parker reviewed for the magazine Constant Reader. From her blog, she appeared to be a fearless teller of truths even if her opinions annoyed people. In reality, Marilyn was a delightful person and even a bit shy out in public and wasn't nearly as bawdy and critical as her blog persona might have indicated. But her online character did something really useful. It weeded out the part of her readership that she didn't want. Anyone that was going to find her writing offensive would automatically stop being a Knitting Curmudgeon blog reader. As Marilyn used to say, "The trash took itself out."

As much as I loved reading Marilyn's blog, the one part of her writing I did not like was when she'd get defensive about a reader's response to something she'd written. When people would leave critical comments or disagree with Marilyn, she'd sometimes take it as a personal attack. To me, it seemed inconsistent to provoke readers and then take their comments or feedback personally.

I ended up aiming for a blog that took the best of the only two other knitting blogs at the time. I posted regularly. I included as much content as I could generate given my speed with knitting, and I posted as many photos as I could manage. I also ginned up controversy to create a self-selecting group of readers that wanted to read what I wrote. An early blog entry in February of 2003 was about online flaming. I took it as an opportunity to let readers know that I had no fear of confrontation in any online environment and that I even relished controversy. To be very clear about who I wanted in my blog-reading community, I also posted the Newcomers' Rules for QueerJoe's Blog. They included the kind of community I was attempting to create among blog readers. It also detailed the demands I had for readers making a comment on a blog post. Mostly, I wanted to make sure that readers/commenters took at least some level of care in what they wrote that would contribute to the vibrancy of my new blog community. I even went so far as to threaten that if they didn't follow the rules, I might edit their comment to include some lascivious thoughts that would make it appear as if they had posted it themselves.

While these rules are no longer posted on the blog, the "internet way back machine" can still find them in full.

I'm sure that you can imagine that there were many people who were really put off by these restrictive rules and insults to the less-inspirational types who might have looked to my blog for inspiration. Unsurprisingly, they were almost the exact population of people I didn't want in my readership. It was incredibly gratifying to have these folks self-select out of participating on my blog.

To be honest, I never actually did any of the things I threatened to do with readers' comments. I also believe that the community of readers who began to regularly read my blog were some of the most interesting, opinionated and enthusiastic readers I could have wished for. That continues to be the case now, over twenty years later.

The rules (and the associated reaction) made me understand that controversy was a useful way of garnering views and new followers very quickly. Often I'd post controversial ideas on queer issues, political ideas or knitting philosophies. If you're not a knitter, you might think that the idea of a controversial knitting philosophy might seem unlikely. But if you really think about how many odd, knee-jerk reactions people on the internet can have, you'll understand how this combination could be possible. Carol, a knitter-friend of mine (and soon-to-be knit-blogger herself) used to characterize controversial knitting topics as the "dog-eat-dog world of knitting."

There was at least one other unexpected benefit of making demands about how readers interacted with the blog. A small group of fiercely loyal readers began to emerge in the comments community. They would support and defend me against anyone trying to attack me or the blog with rude or insulting comments. Some of the defenders were people that I knew before blogging. Others I knew only virtually when it first began. When some readers thought they could attack me via comments, or in various knitting forums, this small cadre of supporters would strike back. I honestly wasn't afraid of attacks. In fact, I welcomed them. More controversy almost always meant more growth in blog readership. However, I grew to value the loyalty of this group of readers.

Their defense of me actually did make it a lot easier to create a blog that was exactly what I wanted it to be. It helped me to carve out and create the precise kind of community I wanted to be a part of.

This new loyalty group and some of the other loyal readers of the blog also had a detrimental effect. At one point, I started to get an oversized ego and believe my own writings, thinking that the persona I presented on QueerJoe was who I really was. A number of times over the years, I had to reassess and remember who I was, or more specifically, how I wanted to portray myself and what my purpose was in blogging. For instance, a regular feature in the blog was a critique of knitting magazines. One designer in particular received much of my criticism. The comments about her work were really mean-spirited and unnecessary. It wasn't until years later that I realized that my platform could have been used to encourage and support the knit-designer community that I valued, rather than tear down those I didn't care for. But sometimes the fabric of community didn't work out quite as I'd hoped, and I had to rip back a little and rework a section.

The other downside of expressing myself publicly in the blog is that readers would sometimes feel they knew me based on my writing. To a certain degree, they did know some aspects of who I was. But they could only get to know the aspects that I presented in the blog. And they often read into my words what they wanted to be true about me as well. This sense of familiarity never had any serious impact on me, but I think often when people got to actually know me, there was some disappointment or surprise at who I was. Frequently, when Marilyn and I would be at a knitting event together, people would remark how much nicer she was in-person and how less nice I was than our blog personae.

The first time I ever really understood how readers viewed me was when I announced that I would be meeting up with other knitters at my local yarn store and then going out for lunch afterwards. I let local readers know that they were welcome to join us. I was totally unprepared for the small mob of people that showed up, but I was also thrilled. About twenty knitters showed up, some traveling for over an hour to participate. We had a great day of yarn shopping, showing off knitting projects, and a nice lunch at a local favorite restaurant of mine.

Over the years, I have loved writing the blog and interacting with the group of people who found their way to QueerJoe. It gave me a vehicle where I could be known by larger and larger groups of people. Like journaling, it provided me a way of clarifying both who I was and who I wanted to be.

Over the ensuing years, blogging platforms began to make it easier and cheaper to publish a blog. More and more knitting blogs were showing up. I would interact with the new knitting blogs that I enjoyed, and link to them and promote them from my platform. These new internet voices would become part of my extended and growing community.

Being an early adopter of blogging within the knitting community, it had been easy to quickly establish a name and a reputation for myself. The small amount of celebrity I found on the internet could also be leveraged to promote someone's new knitting book, or someone selling hand-dyed yarns, or a new yarn store that had opened. I started telling non-knitters that I was considered a minor celebrity in the online knitting community. The word "influencer" hadn't been coined yet as far as I knew, but I did take a lot of satisfaction in having some impact in the knitting world.

One of the only downsides is that I never got accustomed to having people address me in public as "QueerJoe." Behind the safety and anonymity of the internet, it was fine, but when I'd be at a sheep and wool festival, or at a yarn/knitting convention, being addressed as QueerJoe often made me squirm a bit internally. When I was attending a non-knit-related social event and someone would ask me the name of my blog, it always made me feel uneasy to tell them. I mostly put it down to internalized homophobia, though it has gotten easier and easier over the years to say QueerJoe with the pride that it was intended to convey.

Chapter 8
Product Knitter Versus Process Knitter

"We have to remember as adults that we want things done, and as quickly as possible, so that they are finished and out of the way; whereas the child is interested and content in the doing, not the done."

From The Art of Montessori in the Home by Margaret Stephenson

On the Kinsey Scale of product knitter versus process knitter, I am probably a five or six, where a zero is a total product knitter and a six is a complete process knitter.

There have been a number of discussions in various forums about categorizing knitters into one of two types, a product knitter or a process knitter. The idea is that a product knitter enjoys knitting for the purpose of having the final garments or knitting objects that are completed. They'd further be defined as often sticking to a single project until it's finished and only purchasing yarn for a specific project. This group would be inspired by the idea of completing a project. Whereas a process knitter simply enjoys the act of knitting, independent of any specific project. They're happy having multiple projects so that they can ensure their hands are busy whether they're in a doctor's waiting room or sitting in front of the television. The process knitter isn't averse to finishing a project, as long as there's something else in the wings to work on. Yarn purchases of random yarn are common for the process knitter since they will always have options to start a project on a whim with some of their stash yarn.

These are perhaps useful designations to understand more fully what aspect of crafting brings joy and satisfaction in a person's knitting and possibly a way of understanding why knitters behave in different ways. But it's more of a spectrum rather than one or the other.

When I first started writing the blog, someone on the KnitList let me know about a yarn sale they had heard about. A company was selling 180-yard skeins of lightweight, baby alpaca yarn from Peru for a dollar. You could only get the yarn in a natural, drab brown color, but at a dollar, I decided to buy sixty skeins - enough to make a queen-size bedspread.

The yarn was luxuriously soft and the natural poop-brown color eventually grew on me. I got out my finest-gauge needles and cast on 412 stitches and just started to knit a simple stitch pattern that created diagonal rows of eyelets across a mostly solid fabric. Even with the simplicity of the stitch, each row took me about 12 minutes to knit and only added a millimeter of length to the blanket.

With three or four other projects in-progress, the baby alpaca blanket became a filler project - for whenever I wanted something mindless to work on. It quickly became clear that this project was going to take years to complete. It was definitely going to be a lesson in perseverance. On the blog, I began referring to it as my coffin cover to give blog readers an expectation about when it might be finished.

I did end up finishing the coffin cover a few years ago. Once the body of the blanket was as large as I needed it, I gave the edges some durability with a cabled edging. It turned out to be a lovely light-weight bed blanket that adds the perfect amount of warmth as we transition to chillier evenings in the Fall.

There are two other behaviors that demonstrate that I'm more about the process than the finished product. First, I don't mind unraveling work to fix a mistake. Second, I am much more inspired to take on a new project if I'm learning a new technique. When I was a new knitter, the thought of ripping back hours of work was daunting. Once I got to the point in my experience as a knitter where I was more comfortable with knitting and began to enjoy the rhythmic, repetitive nature of it, the dread of going back to fix a mistake went away. Also, if I see an interesting stitch pattern, or a new technique for making cables, I'm all in for the enjoyment of the process.

There are also some characteristics of my knitting that demonstrate I'm a product-knitter as well. First, I'm sometimes impatient to get to the end of a project. Especially a larger project or a project with a deadline, such as a birthday gift. I push myself to power-knit until I reach specific milestones for the project. I often start to get tired of the color of the yarn and I'll also start to question whether I even like the garment I'm making. When non-knitters find out that I knit, they often remark how much patience I must have. They often confuse patience and perseverance. I don't consider myself very patient as I push myself to get to the next row, or the next color stripe in a project. But it's almost inconceivable to me that I'd give up on a project that I care about. There's rarely any question as to whether I will continue working on a project until it's completed. Even a project that might take years. The second product-knitter characteristic only appeared when I started selling some of my knit designs at local craft shows. When I needed to put together an inventory of knitted hats and scarfs to display and sell, not only did I have a deadline, but I had certain minimum inventory numbers I had to have ready for each show. Production knitting for craft shows was a very different activity than leisure knitting, and I much prefer when I can enjoy the process.

Not surprisingly, my predilection toward process versus product carried over into the fabric-making of community as well. Refining, trying new things, eliciting feedback and constantly making changes to the space where community formed have all become my standard. For me, the formation of community is definitely more of a journey than a destination.

Chapter 9
Two Sides to Being a Man Who Knits

"I like to just think of myself as a normal person who just has a passion, has a goal and a dream and goes out and does it. And that's really how I've always lived my life."

Michael Phelps

Being a man who knits is one of the experiences that made me feel like an outsider in at least two different ways. For many of the guy-knitters, our gender both separated many of us from the general community of knitters, but it also increased the gravitational pull toward each other. So, it's an integral component to the eventual creation of what has become my chosen community.

The experience of many men who participate in fiber arts was that they were treated in one of two ways by others in the crafting world. They were either treated as outsiders who were not fully welcome into a women's enclave. Or they were fawned over as if they were some special, sparkling unicorn with magical qualities because they were audacious enough to take up knitting.

First let me honestly admit that I've benefited from both of those two reactions.

Being warned off from people that didn't want me was a useful way to select or opt out of a group or community where I wasn't welcome. Also, when I started participating in online forums and blogging, the haters became an important way of promoting myself. Having people that publicly criticized me gave me a focal point for gathering defenders who rallied to my defense. Controversy is one of the easiest ways to establish a following and haters were the most effective tool for ginning up high levels of controversy.

Being treated in an unwarranted, special way gave me more access to some parts of the fiber world than I might have had otherwise. The overly politically-correct folks could point to their support of me as a badge of their own honor. When I started selling my knitwear at local craft shows, it was almost always a big selling point that it was not just hand-knit, but hand-knit by a man! My efforts at designing were also afforded a more positive response because of my sex. It's completely unmerited, but men's efforts in most areas are taken more seriously…even in areas that are typically seen as a women's domain.

There were many examples of how I was treated in both ways. There were also many in the knitting community that just treated me like a standard, run-of-the-mill knitter.

One of the more obvious examples of being treated as an unwelcome member of the knitting world was when I took a part-time job on Sundays at the Tomato Factory yarn store. I was working by myself one Sunday, and a phone call came in. The woman calling had some questions about ordering yarn from one of the recent mailers she'd received. She asked to speak with Liz (the owner). I told her she wasn't in and offered to help her. She then asked to speak with Carol, who worked there. I again told her that she wasn't in and I'd be happy to help. When she asked to speak with a third female staff member, I realized what she was looking for. Or specifically, I realized what she wasn't looking for. I let her know the owner and the two staff members she asked about would be back in the store on Tuesday morning, but that I was the only person in the store today. She ended the call, saying she would call back then.

It was a bit frustrating to know that I could have helped her. But I also realized that some people didn't think I belonged in this world, or didn't think I could offer the kind of assistance they needed because I was a man. I also understood that this didn't damage me in any way. In this particular case, it just postponed when this knitter would get her yarn.

I feel like somewhat of a whiner complaining about this treatment. Women have long been dismissed in typically male-dominated fields for years and they know exactly what my experience was like. But for me, it was a new experience that opened my eyes to a broad range of understanding about how ignorant and short-sighted gender stereotypes and biases can be.

I have also been ridiculed by men for being a knitter. One time I invited my boss to my house for dinner and when he asked why there were knitting needles and yarn in my living room, I told him that I was a knitter. He was also a gay man, so for some reason I assumed this wouldn't be a controversial statement about myself. He mocked me for about five minutes for having such a sissy hobby until he realized that I didn't care about his thoughts on the matter.

In fact, he realized I was quite proud of how proficient I was when I showed him some of the things I'd made. It was easy to see that his comments about my knitting were saying much more about his own uncertainties about his manhood than about mine.

I honestly don't have any hard feelings for anyone that disparages me because of my knitting or that I don't conform to their gender expectations. Again, women have been dismissed (or worse) for years by ignorant men for taking on "men's work." Having grown up as a more sensitive man than is perhaps the norm, I'm quite thick-skinned and used to it. In fact, I actually expected this kind of reaction to a certain extent, so it wasn't a surprise when it happened.

What did surprise me was the unwarranted praise and attribution of knitting skills to me that either weren't true, or weren't demonstrated so that the person praising me could have possibly known them to be true. I called it the "some of my best friends are men who knit" phenomenon. Being praised for doing something because I was a man seemed like someone's overreaction to make sure everyone knew that they were completely open-minded and that they weren't discriminatory, hateful or exclusionary in any way. There had been similar experiences as a gay man where I was often attributed with better taste or a more keen sense of aesthetics simply because I was a gay man.

It's more difficult to pinpoint specific instances where I was granted special privileges for being a male knitter. Disdain is a lot easier to identify than unwarranted privilege. I do honestly think that there are many male knitwear designers who get much more attention than they merit compared to their female counterparts - including me.

It also seemed that the distinction of being a male knitter helped me establish myself within the knitting community more easily. I was oftentimes accorded more importance than I deserved. My advice and answers to knitting questions seemed to get more credence.

There were even non-knitters who found it noteworthy that I was a man who knit. About ten years ago, I was being interviewed for a gay radio show with two other men who knit. Harry, the radio show host had briefed us before the show that we couldn't swear or say anything lewd during the interview as it was live with only a few-second delay which made it very difficult to bleep out anything. But when one of his questions was marveling that men had taken up this hobby and then he asked if men bring anything particularly special to the craft, did we do anything different as men to make knitted fabric, there was a pause with the three knitters. I responded that as men, we didn't use anything except knitting needles just like all other knitters. The tone of my reply indicated to Harry that I was heading in a dangerous direction with this line of questioning, so he quickly switched to a different topic.

The rationale for being fawned over perhaps had multiple factors. Did the über-supportive folks find me attractive and it was more flirting than fawning? Was my energy and enthusiasm just more contagious? Was just the fact that I was a cis-gendered, white man granting me some level of entitlement in the world of knitting? Probably all of these had some impact on my easy acceptance into the knitting communities. But talk to any man who's been knitting for a while and ask them if they've experienced undue praise and encouragement for just being a man and I'll bet they'll know exactly what you're talking about.

Whatever the rationale for either way I was treated, the reactions to being despised and adored is a very strange phenomenon. They both made me feel like an outsider.

Chapter 10
Knitting and Wool Events

"Surround yourself with a bunch of like-minded people, and you'll soak up their habits like a starved sponge."

Vir Das

Yarn "Conventions"

As part of working at the two yarn stores, I helped participate in a knitting convention (of sorts) called Stitches. Stitches was an annual event on the East coast of the States sponsored by a popular knitting magazine. Both the event and the magazine are now defunct, but not before growing into a significantly large event. There was eventually a Stitches East, Stitches West, Stitches Midwest, and maybe even some others. Vogue Knitting Magazine continues to sponsor a similar event that is extremely popular with knitters, designers and yarn/fiber vendors.

At the time, Stitches would sell booth space to yarn vendors to populate the marketplace where attendees could purchase yarn, knitting tools, books, patterns and anything related to fiber crafts. It would also bring together well-known fiber artists to present workshops on various topics or techniques of interest. Prior to the proliferation of internet sales, yarn stores had very little way of promoting themselves to a nationwide audience. The market at Stitches provided that. The event would happen in large convention centers and would attract an enormous group of people.

Registering for the highly sought-after workshops became almost competitive. And bragging rights on various knitting forums were popular when someone made their way into a particularly popular class. Workshop instructors became the major celebrities in this booming community. Especially if the workshop leader had knitting books published or published a popular blog.

Announcing that I would be attending various yarn conventions on my blog, allowed readers to meet me in-person. It also allowed me to get together with a loose-forming community of knitters and knit-bloggers and celebrate the craft that brought us together. It was really the first time I ever understood how large and varied the yarn-loving universe could be. I also started understanding my place in that universe. Walking around the various vendor booths and chatting with well-known designers, bloggers, vendors and instructors felt like I was truly in my element. I think "minor celebrity" continued to be an apt description.

Sheep & Wool Festivals

The other type of gatherings that brought together knitters and yarn-vendors were the regional sheep and wool festivals. Typically, these events took place on county fairgrounds where other similar agricultural events would happen, like 4-H and rural county fairs. The two big sheep and wool festivals on the East Coast were the Maryland Sheep & Wool Festival which takes place in early May each year in West Friendship, Maryland, and the New York State Sheep & Wool Festival which takes place each October in Rhinebeck, New York.

Like Stitches and Vogue Knitting Live, both sheep and wool festival events bring together many fiber-related vendors. Wool mills, book publishers, independent yarn dyers, spinning wheel companies, sheep farmers, and of course, yarn companies and stores. Vendors purchase booth space in one of the multiple barn buildings on the festival grounds. These festivals are a great way of getting to touch and feel yarn in-person. Which helped a lot as yarn sales were starting to become more available online. Fiber-arts is obviously a very tactile activity, so buying yarn without being able to touch it, or see the actual color of it was one of the obstacles of selling it online. But once you had the chance to shop for a specific brand of yarn in-person, you could purchase it online with more assurance that it would be what you wanted for a project or a specific purpose.

The festivals were also a great way of showing off the skills of talented independent yarn dyers. Boutique yarn businesses that didn't have the resources to expand broadly and were typically only found in regional stores could now have a broader audience.

If you were one of the people who also spun their own yarns, you had access to an amazing array of beautiful, unspun fibers, prize fleeces from the local farmers and tools, such as drop-spindles, drum carders, niddy-noddies, and spinning wheels.

Around 2002 or 2003, I had added yarn-spinning to my growing slate of fiber-related skills. So it was fantastic to be able to shop for roving - which is wool that has been cleaned and fluffed up to make it ready to be spun into yarn, and also try out different spinning wheels and purchase books and other tools for spinning.

I started regularly attending the New York State Sheep & Wool Festival (known as Rhinebeck) in 2003. It gave me the opportunity to meet up with blog readers, other bloggers and knit-friends from the various online forums. It started to become an annual get-together for a group of about eight to ten of us. Often, after a day of shopping for anything fiber-related, we'd head to a nearby diner and discuss the day and those items we'd found and any purchases of yarn or wool.

In 2004, the annual Rhinebeck meet-up group started talking about a new knit blogger in Chicago, Franklin Habit. Franklin was just starting to garner some well-deserved attention in the virtual knitting community. He's a brilliantly clever writer and we all started reading his blog faithfully. We also wanted to support his success in the fiber world in any way we could. Many of us linked to his blog and we promoted his blog on various forums. One of the many reasons for the popularity of his blog was that he had a recurring cartoon character, Dolores, who was a bawdy sheep, who drank, smoked, swore, caroused and did and said the types of things that the blog author was much too refined to ever do or say himself. Franklin is a very talented artist as well as a writer and often delighted his readers with cartoon drawings of Dolores in wonderfully different scenarios. Just like the sharp-tongued ventriloquist dummy who could get away with saying insulting things to an audience whilst protecting the ventriloquist who was actually saying the words, Dolores said many of the things we all wanted to say.

But we also wanted to meet Franklin. Chicago isn't exactly local to Rhinebeck, so we started to discuss ways we could get to meet Franklin and have him somehow become part of our group. A blog reader suggested that I should sponsor a blog fundraiser to fly him in for Rhinebeck in 2005. I ran the idea by Franklin and he loved it. So, the "Fresh-Air Group for Franklin" (FAG for Franklin was its short-lived name) was born. We needed about $800 to cover his travel and lodging costs, and I wasn't sure I was influential enough to have this be a successful fundraiser. So, we offered prizes to be raffled off for any donations of a certain amount. Knitting books, yarn, sets of double-pointed knitting needles. We had about a half dozen prizes, many of them donated by blog readers who also wanted to meet Franklin.

Surprisingly, lots of people donated to the fund very quickly. Within a week, we had enough money to fly Franklin into Philadelphia for a weekend and have him stay at a local bed & breakfast near me. I shuttled him to and from the airport and up to Rhinebeck that week. He was as delightful in-person as we had imagined from his writings and like many of us, I was truly grateful for having gotten the chance to meet him. Many of the people in our knitting circles were very enthused by an event that would bring us all together. We got to see scores of people that Saturday in Rhinebeck. People who, up until that point we had never met in-person.

Rhinebeck was starting to be the launchpad where a community was coming into finer focus. The annual gathering started to be a catalyst for joining wayward individuals into a more and more tightly-knit community.

Chapter 11
The Spark - A Confluence of Events

"A thrumming of piano-strings beyond the gardens and through the elms. At length the melody steals into my being. I know not when it began to occupy me. By some fortunate coincidence of thought or circumstance I am attuned to the universe, I am fitted to hear, my being moves in a sphere of melody, my fancy and imagination are excited to an inconceivable degree. This is no longer the dull earth on which I stood."

Henry David Thoreau

Looking back at all the paths that got me to where I was at that point in my life, I could probably have easily seen where it would lead. But I didn't take that opportunity of looking for the trajectory of my identity and my desire to be part of a community. I just kept moving forward in the general direction of those areas that brought me joy.

Two other factors needed to be in place to have the right environment for an amazing and transformational experience to take place.

Easton Mountain Retreat Center

In 2007, I was on a long-term work assignment in Schenectady, New York. I was working for a consulting company helping large corporations implement software to help them manage their employees. Specifically, my expertise was in the module of a complex software that enabled large companies to manage their employee benefits. While I was living in Eastern Pennsylvania at the time, I would drive up to Schenectady each week on Monday morning and stay at a hotel in the area. I'd drive home on Thursday evening to spend my weekends at home with Thaddeus. On and off, this assignment lasted for over 9 years, so I was frequently in Upstate New York.

On some of the more critical time periods during our projects, I was required to work through the weekend and stay in Upstate NY for two consecutive weeks. Often, on these two-week stints I needed to be available and close by, but not necessarily physically present at the client site. So when things went well on those infrequent weekends and I wasn't required to attend to some urgent issue, I was always looking for something entertaining to do.

During some of my free time up there, I had been participating in a social group (unrelated to knitting) and met someone who would become a friend. Stephen was an adventurous guy who had moved to Upstate NY from the Pacific Northwest to work at a retreat center called Easton Mountain. He also co-hosted a weekly radio show called Quest of Life on the local college radio station, which is where my two knitter friends and I were eventually interviewed as men who knit. His co-host, Harry would interview someone in the LGBTQ+ world in the first hour, and then Stephen would play music by LGBTQ+ artists in the second hour.

On one of the weekends where I was required to stay in Upstate NY, Stephen said that Easton Mountain was having a community barbecue that Saturday and that I should come. Since Easton was both his workplace and his residence, Stephen had been building a cabin on the retreat property and was very excited and proud of how it was proceeding. I was eager to see his accomplishments and progress. I knew I'd have spare time, so I accepted and looked forward to going.

For those of you unfamiliar with Upstate New York, there are some very rural areas. Easton Mountain is in an area that is definitely not like New York City and/or any of the more populated areas of the State. I had never seen the retreat center where Stephen worked, but I heard it was quite beautiful. It's on the southeastern edge of the Adirondack Mountains near the border of Vermont.

That Saturday, work was quiet and I wasn't needed in the office. I headed out to Greenwich, New York (pronounced green-witch, unlike the Village in New York City). One thing about me is that I have a terrible sense of direction and I hate getting lost. So, I made sure that I had been given very detailed directions to Easton Mountain. Unfortunately, those directions were missing one turn and I got terribly lost. Honestly, I have no idea how lost I was, it was terrible simply because I was lost. I found myself in a rural area with lots of farming and with very few houses and virtually no businesses. I pulled off on a side road to see if I could figure out where I was going. Fortunately, as I did, I saw a dirt driveway with two guys behind a pick-up truck in the driveway. I asked if they knew where Easton Mountain was? I got a little panicky when they said they had never heard of it. They asked me if it was the ski mountain, Willard Mountain. I was pretty certain it wasn't. They were just about to end the conversation, when one of them asked if it was the old nudist resort, The Phoenix. Somewhere, in the back of my mind, I remember Stephen had said it used to be a nudist camp. To my great relief, they were able to fill in the missing turn and tell me how to get there.

I arrived at the main lodge of Easton Mountain about 10 minutes later. I was a bit frazzled from the panic of being lost. Stephen met me and took me on a tour of the property. The main buildings are in front of a large, beautiful pond which is directly in front of the twin, rounded peaks of Easton Mountain (from that elevation, they really look more like large hills, but they're still quite beautiful). He showed me the cabin he was building and introduced me to some of the guys at Easton Mountain.

I was immediately enamored with everything about the place.

It was early June and the weather was perfect. Partly cloudy, but mostly blue skies and temperatures that didn't even require a jacket. It is also a very lush time of year in that area and the trees and bushes were thick and dense where land hadn't been cleared. Where it had been cleared, the grassy areas were deep green and thick. There were trails all over the property that cut through most of the dense, forested areas.

Stephen had some work errands to attend to, and I was left to my own devices for an hour or so before the community barbecue began. So, I decided to go on an exploratory hike by myself around the property.

If I had to categorize myself as a city guy or a country guy, I'd probably say that I was more of a suburban guy. I am not typically one of those people that is energized by being in nature. I'm also not one who feels like the place where I am, is the reason for my joy or well-being. I usually find that my circumstances aren't the main factor in determining how good or bad I feel about an experience.

But this experience was very different. I walked through a very small percentage of the 175-acre property, but it reminded me of the times when I'd take an adventure to the local fishing pond when I was young…checking out the frog streams, and the flowers and staying clear of dragonflies (because they always seemed dangerous to me). The sense of freedom and serenity I experienced while wandering aimlessly was overwhelming and I can recall that feeling even as I write this now, over 15 years later. I can still recall the smells of the moist earth and the forest bed in my mind's nose right now.

Perhaps it was the juxtaposition of feeling panicked and lost and then being submerged in the serenity of nature that made it such a highly contrasted and wonderful experience. Whatever the reason, I recall thinking that I would need to figure out some way of coming back to Easton Mountain. The remainder of my time there that day made me understand why natural spas had sprung up in that area, such as Saratoga Springs. I felt rejuvenated and restored to some sense of equilibrium that I hadn't even noticed had been out of balance.

When I got back to my hotel room in Schenectady, I checked out the retreat schedule on the Easton Mountain web site to see if there was any event or retreat that Thaddeus and I might consider attending. But most events just didn't sound like something we'd enjoy. Despite that, the gravitational pull of Easton Mountain became a part of the overall pull toward my eventual community.

KnitterGuyTed

Edward Myatt, who went by Ted, was a knitter and blogger in Ontario, Canada. He was a very experienced knitter with a vast amount of knowledge in every area of the craft. He was steeped in the history of knitting and would often be able to provide detailed and useful answers to questions on various online forums. For instance, he understood why plied yarn was twisted in a specific direction and which yarn-twist direction worked best with knitting versus crochet. He could always add some level of understanding when questions or debates on the knitting forums came up.

Ted ended up focusing most of his knitting expertise in the area of knitted lace. Lace knitting is almost a craft unto itself with an extensive history of different cultures making their own versions of lace. Estonian lace shawls, wedding ring shawls from the Shetland Islands, Alaskan native lace design, Victorian lace, etc. Ted characterized all of his knitting and design work as reflecting a love of "knitterly history" with a modern twist. I would have added that Ted himself had an old-fashioned quality of looking at life and its events with a simple clarity that was unfettered by complex social filters. He would often post seemingly naive questions about a topic that would require anyone responding to look at the root of an issue and think more deeply about it than they might have otherwise.

Ted worked for a Canadian agency associated with unemployment/workforce training, and he had very specific ideas about how things should go there. The clarity with which he saw most things made it obvious to him how things ought to work. As is often the case with employers, they didn't always see it the same way. From our conversations, I often got the feeling that Ted didn't feel very appreciated by his employer. Most of his self-esteem came through his participation in the fiber world he had cultivated.

Ted was also a spinner (someone that can turn wool into yarn). He could spin yarn on a wheel, but he was also very proficient at using a drop-spindle. There are many types of drop-spindles, but they are usually somewhat small, made of wood and resemble a spinning top, like an old child's toy. They're made to spin like a top, so they can add twist to wool or other fiber to form it into yarn. While the drop-spindle tool is more portable than a spinning wheel, it also doesn't hold as much spun yarn. So, the process of making yarn is more time-consuming on a drop-spindle. Though, Ted would often debate that last statement with me.

Ted made some of the finest gauge, lace yarns on his drop spindle. He once gifted me with one of his very large skeins of very fine, thin yarns. In addition to being truly beautiful, it knit up to an even more beautiful fabric. Even though I also spin yarn, it was unfathomable for me to imagine having created hundreds of meters of this lace-weight yarn on a drop-spindle. There aren't many who I consider to have more perseverance when it comes to fiber arts, than I do, but Ted was one of them.

Over the years, the KnitList which was now on the Yahoo Groups platform had broken out into many spin-off groups…Sock knitters, LGBT Knitters, Men Who Knit. Ted and I were in mostly the same forums, so I got to virtually know him after years of reading his posts. When our Rhinebeck group started to form, he became a part of our annual meetup.

The Confluence

What do Easton Mountain, knitting conventions, sheep and wool festivals, and Ted have to do with each other?

In the Autumn of 2007, I announced on my blog and on various knitting forums that I planned to be at Rhinebeck as in prior years. Other than the joy of getting to see my fiber friends, there was nothing extraordinary about this year's visit. Selma, Ted, Carol, Lars, Kathy and Marilyn were there. Plus Véronik, a very talented knitwear designer from Canada joined our pack that year.

I was considering buying a fleece and a drum carder (a device for brushing shorn wool to prepare it to be spun into yarn), so at lunch that day, I sat down with Ted to solicit his thoughts and just take a moment to catch up with him. Ted introduced me to Dave, a relatively new knitter who was a staff member at a retreat center where Ted had recently been. I inquired more about the retreat center and was astounded to find out that it was Easton Mountain.

I felt the first jolt of excitement that someone else in my world had experienced this beautiful place. That excitement continued to grow as Ted described a similar feeling as I'd had at Easton Mountain - the rich, verdant beauty and serenity of the place. I hadn't realized how much I wanted to share my experience of Easton until I was actually sharing it with someone else who had also been there.

Adding to the coincidence, after my friend Stephen had left Easton Mountain, Dave had taken over the cabin that Stephen had built and was now living there as his staff residence.

Ted had been at a week-long retreat at Easton Mountain during the summer of 2007 and was knitting in front of the guesthouse. Dave had just taught himself to knit. He was still in the early phase of self-identification where finding other similarly-inclined people was exhilarating. He approached Ted to ask him what he was knitting and struck up a friendship. In addition to telling Dave about Rhinebeck, he also mentioned that Easton Mountain would be a nice place to have a small group of guys get together and hang out in the sunroom and knit.

I was fully re-energized and excited again by recalling the memory of my visit to Easton Mountain. I was also reminded of just how much I wanted to get back there again. So, when Ted mentioned that he envisioned a group of guys getting together at Easton Mountain for a knitting retreat, it all came together in an instant. It was as if all the correct atoms came together in an environment that was supportive of fusing in a powerful way. My own little big bang at the initial creation of a new community.

Chapter 12
The Initial Forming of Community

"To confer the gift of drawing, we must create an eye that sees, a hand that obeys, a soul that feels; and in this task, the whole life must cooperate. In this sense, life itself is the only preparation for drawing. Once we have lived, the inner spark of vision does the rest."

Maria Montessori

The big-bang took place in October of 2007. But like many atomic reactions, there was no stopping the chain-reaction once it began.

Being from Canada, Ted wanted to participate in organizing a men's knitting event at Easton Mountain. Being outside this country limited his ability to do many of the tasks associated with organizing such an event. That's where I jumped in with great eagerness. I told him I'd be glad to handle getting it all set up and working with Dave at Easton Mountain to arrange it all, and work with him along the way. We agreed that we'd like to organize something for a weekend in May of 2008. I told Dave I'd contact him at Easton Mountain to arrange for dates.

To be very clear, while Ted, Dave and I were excited about the possibility of a small get-together of guys knitting at Easton Mountain, we really didn't think it would be momentous. During the planning session with Dave, he asked us how many guys we expected to register. Ted estimated that through announcing this on his blog and my blog and various knitting forums that we'd probably get about eight to ten guys interested in attending. I had a somewhat more optimistic idea of ten to twelve guys.

Over the course of the next few weeks, Ted and I corresponded to work out many of the details. We settled on the name, Men's Spring Knitting Retreat and quickly got used to the acronym MSKR. But we decided that the event was open to any man interested in any fiber-related activity. We also thought we'd allow any attendees to invite their same-sex partners to join them, even if they weren't into knitting, crochet, embroidery, weaving, spinning, or any yarn-related activity.

I contacted Dave at Easton shortly after Rhinebeck and we discussed possible weekends in May. For the third weekend in May, they had tentatively scheduled two other small groups at Easton Mountain, so he thought it would be a good slot for our small group. We scheduled a Friday-Sunday booking which included lodging and meals from Friday dinner to Sunday lunch that would cost the participants the standard rate at Easton Mountain for 2 nights and meals. There were no additional upcharges for any retreat-related activities. Easton Mountain would handle the registration/booking and organize the rooming assignments, dietary requirements and sending out a data sheet about the retreat center and directions on how to get there. They would also have Dave be the retreat liaison to go through ground rules, safety regulations and other sundry items that the guys would want to know about. We also agreed that Dave, or any guys who worked or volunteered at Easton Mountain who were interested in attending could attend the retreat as a participant.

In reality, Ted and I basically set a date to meet up at Easton Mountain. We were simply going to let any interested guys know about it as well so they could make arrangements to join us if they cared to. It was initially intended to be a somewhat informal get-together. There was a flurry of correspondence between Ted and I and we decided that we needed to put together a web page and a flier. We also thought we should coordinate how and what we communicated in our respective blogs and on knitting forums. I went to work on the web site and the flier. This started with trying to come up with a logo or some visual symbol.

Unfortunately, as much as I love and appreciate color and design, I don't have a lot of talent or creativity when it comes to designing graphics. I settled on taking a photo of a skein of yarn with two walnut, hand-turned knitting needles stuck into it. It was somewhat trite and uncreative for a logo, but I hoped that the success of the event wouldn't hinge on the uninspired choice of graphics.

I also searched through all of my blog photos for any fiber-related photos that showed men socializing around knitting, spinning, etc. I had surprisingly few to choose from. For a man who blogged about knitting, I was disappointed that I had virtually no photos of men knitting. Franklin had taken a beautiful photo of me learning how to use a new, custom-made spinning wheel at Rhinebeck. The wheel maker, Gil, was a guy, so it was really the only photo that had more than one guy doing something fiber-related. I also stole a photo from Easton Mountain's website and used a couple of other blog photos of me knitting.

Having never organized even a small retreat, I didn't know what to worry about. I didn't know what I didn't know. That always makes me somewhat anxious. Each time a new question came up about the event, Ted and I would discuss it and come up with how we thought it should be addressed. But the thought that we were creating something out of nothing was also incredibly energizing and exciting. It often surprises me to realize how closely related anxiety and excitement are when it comes to experiencing them.

One of the benefits of having a committee of two (three, if you include all the advice we got from Dave as well), we established foundational rules for this event that we continue to follow and add to each year.

Finally, after getting it all scheduled and documented on the internet and in a PDF flier, we went public on December 7, 2007. Ted and I posted a blog entry describing the basics and a link to the new web page. We also posted to online forums such as Men Who Knit and LGBT Knitters to let them know about the event.

While Ted didn't ever seem to get overly excited, he and I were both tingling with the exhilaration of having made this thing happen. In reality, once the idea was voiced by Ted, it was almost as though we had just jumped off a ledge. It was inevitable that we would land. But this step in the process just seemed to indicate that our landing wouldn't be catastrophic. It might not be great, but it wasn't going to be a crash landing.

There were basically two reactions to my blog entry announcement. Most of the blog readers were women, so the biggest reaction came from them. In general, they felt left out. They expressed it in different ways. The spectrum went from exuberant joy for us with a tinge of envy, to deeply hurt and angry that we had been exclusionary. Fortunately, there were very few on the latter end of that spectrum. But Ted and I felt we needed to address this response.

The general answer we came up with was that there were a number of retreats for all knitters (that were usually all women) and we highly encouraged them to look into those events. But more importantly, Ted and I wanted everyone to understand that the purpose of having a men's retreat wasn't to be exclusionary. The purpose of the retreat was to celebrate the men's knitting community. Yes, it meant excluding women from the event, but exclusivity wasn't the purpose. To us, that was a big difference.

There's another similar situation where I was accustomed to differentiating between celebrating and excluding. There are groups, for instance, that call for having a "straight pride" parade during June since many LGBTQIA+ groups have pride parades during that month. Clearly, heterosexuals are not a group that needs to declare their pride in the face of a history of discrimination and being made to feel lesser-than the rest of society. It seems clear that the purpose of a straight pride parade is not to celebrate a population, but to be divisive and antagonistic.

The LGBTQIA+ population doesn't exclude people when they organize an event that celebrates who they are, and the pride they experience in being who they are.

The conversation of exclusion versus celebration isn't meant to change hearts and minds, it's simply to show that we went through a process to clarify our intentions. Clarifying our purpose was very useful, even if there's still some disagreement about where we landed on this issue.

The second response was mostly from men in fiber-crafts. They loved the idea and wanted to participate.

Being one in the second group, I called and registered immediately. Often events like this begin the moment that you register. The excitement builds and every email confirmation or piece of information received between registration and the actual event helps to build the level of engagement and excitement. You can imagine how many times I thought back to my short time at Easton Mountain and imagined myself walking through the beauty of the place again. I was very eager to return.

Ted also sent out an email a few days after the blog posts to a list of guys whose email addresses we had. We had arranged with Dave that he would send us a spreadsheet with the list of participants to give us a sense about who and what to expect. Initially, there was enough space at Easton Mountain to accommodate about twelve of us in between the other two retreats that weekend.

Then suddenly, it got really exciting and a bit terrifying as well. About three weeks after we opened registration, Dave called me and told me we had to stop promoting the event. They had 25 guys registered for the retreat and no more spots open for that weekend. I went into a bit of a panic. It seemed as though it had gotten more real than any of us had expected it to. I quickly contacted Ted and he kind of chuckled as he said, "I guess that means we're going to have to put together an official agenda of things to do for this large of a group." I was glad Ted was the more emotionally stable of the two of us because his calm kept me less panicked.

On a more immediate basis, Dave set up a waiting list for the event and took down the contact information for anyone hoping to attend. Dave also ended up rescheduling one of the other two events slated for that weekend since it didn't look like it was going to have enough registrations to make it viable.

Ted and I went to work on scheduling activities for the weekend. We started by reaching out to the guys who had registered and asked if they'd like to present a workshop. We had no funds to pay for workshop leaders, and Ted and I both knew we could present a workshop on some fiber-related topic. We also hoped one or two of the other guys could as well. Turns out that we had quite a few willing and eager guys looking to lead workshops. We ended up having scheduled workshops on a variety of topics, including double-knitting, spinning cotton fiber, beginner lace-knitting (Ted's specialty), men's sock design, introduction to cables, turning a knitted heel, and a workshop on different ways of binding off. I also included a workshop on beginner spinning to introduce any new, would-be spinners to another skill.

We started to use a newly created social media platform for fiber arts, called Ravelry to send out informal communications to the attendees and any guys interested in the retreat. We set up a forum, and invited anyone to participate. This gave us an even broader access to guys around the world. It sparked the interest of guys from Boston, San Francisco, Canada, Florida, and even as far as the United Kingdom, Australia and New Zealand. It also gave us more exposure to the fiber-vendor community. Both independent and larger commercial yarn companies offered to donate items to the retreat in exchange for promoting their product to the men's knitting community. We asked each of the donors to include 40 business cards or promotional fliers with their donation so that we could make sure each guy could patronize the businesses that had supported the retreat.

We also looked for a fiber-related road trip we could arrange that was local to Easton Mountain. As luck would have it, there was an alpaca farm about ten minutes from the retreat center who would have just had their Spring birthing of baby alpacas. They were willing to host a visit from a group of guy-knitters. Now we had a very healthy agenda to offer the guys. It also turned out that closing one of the events scheduled for that weekend at Easton Mountain opened up more spots for MSKR. We ended up having 32 guys register for the retreat. The number was significant enough to make us start thinking of the retreat as an annual event. Not just a one-time event.

During this period of time, I had taken on a new project in Wilmington, Delaware. They were just beginning their project, so my work didn't keep me overly busy. I had plenty of spare time to work on planning the retreat. I decided to get incredibly organized about readying for the retreat. I set up a spreadsheet listing all the attendees and got to work on fleshing out the rest of the agenda. The agenda now had a basic structure of registration/check-in, meals, workshops, morning yoga, a show and tell night, and a road trip.

But the workshop section was going to be more complex than initially expected. The volunteer workshop leaders had limits on the number of guys in each of their workshops, so we needed a method of determining interest levels for each workshop and assigning the guys into desired workshop sessions. I looked for some web-form functionality to collect this information, but none of the existing web-survey companies allowed me to make the exact kind of questionnaire I needed. I decided to teach myself PHP programming. PHP is a scripting language that allows for the creation of web forms, collection of submitted information in a database and querying the resulting database. I already had some of the database querying skills, so I understood some of the language already. But it took me about a week to get a working web form to send out to the attendees. It was so incredibly satisfying to be able to put my aptitude for technology into something I was passionate about.

I also needed some information from them for an ice-breaker idea I had in mind. Like many people, I hate ice-breakers. They seem so forced and unnatural. But I had a really good one that didn't feel so awkward. I asked each attendee to provide us with three random facts about themselves. "I have a butterfly tattoo on my inner thigh." "My birthday is the same as Emmylou Harris." "Every morning my cat and dog sit together on the side of the bed until I get up and feed them." I created an Excel Spreadsheet that created individual BINGO cards with these random factoids about the participants. Each guy got a BINGO card that excluded their own bits of trivia, so they could search through the group of attendees to find enough matches to get a BINGO.

We added some incentive for playing. The faster they got a BINGO, the higher priority ranking they got at choosing their prize from the large table of donated yarn and knit-related items. We had collected about 40 different donations of fiber-related prizes for the swag table, so each of the guys would definitely get some prize.

I sent out the first "big email" to the 32 scheduled participants asking them to confirm their personal information, complete the workshop request form and to provide me with random facts about themselves. My first indicator that this was going to be a supportive community was that I got responses from all 32 guys within a week.

Now I could assign workshops, begin creating individualized agendas, and create personalized BINGO cards for each of the guys.

Finally, I wanted to have some token giveaways to present to the guys when they registered. Any giveaways had to be inexpensive, since we had no budget to purchase gifts, especially when the cost for each was multiplied by 40 since we didn't know the final total count until the week of the event.

I had to get creative about frugally putting together a set of items to give away to the guys attending the retreat. I scoured various Dollar Store outlets, office-supply stores and even hardware stores to look for things I could get for a maximum of $1 each. I ended up finding 40 funky, fabric, cross-shoulder bags in one of the dollar stores. They were made of a thin, cotton fabric, but they came in darker colors that I thought would make great little project-bags for small, men's knitted projects, like a pair of socks. I also found inexpensive pens and notepads to include in the project-bags. Finally, a friend who worked for M&M Mars offered to donate some candy. They donated both individual candy bars to include in the guys' bags as well as ten pounds of M&Ms for snacking during the retreat.

We were in constant communications with the guys either through emails or on various Ravelry forums to make sure everyone had everything they needed. It seemed like an eternity from when we first opened registration in December to when the retreat would actually happen and we wanted to keep the guys engaged as much as possible and energized about attending.

Then all of a sudden it was late April and the retreat was only weeks away. I had my first sleepless night worrying about anything and everything that might happen or items that I might forget. I'm not normally a very detail-oriented person. But my work as a project manager made me realize that creating a detailed project plan was one of the easiest ways to help assure that events would be successful. So, I created a project plan. Not only did I document the tasks that I needed to accomplish and when, but I also documented all the tasks that had already been completed. Having a detailed list of all that we had completed and all that needed to be done made me feel a little more at ease with it all. It also helped prepare me for future years if this first event went well.

Chapter 13
Creating The Most Wonderfully Tight-Knit Fabric

*"The way
You alchemize
a soulless world
into a sacred
world is by
treating everyone
as if they are
sacred, until
the sacred in them
remembers."*

Sarah Durham Wilson

My hope for everyone is that they get to experience the same kind of feeling I had when I realized I could take two sticks and some yarn and turn it into fabric. It was profoundly satisfying. There are many routes to this feeling of satisfaction that I wish all to experience, but knitting brought me to it. It was similarly satisfying to witness the guys arrive and assemble into an amazingly loving and supportive community at the first ever Men's Knitting Retreat in May of 2008.

The last few weeks before the retreat sped by very quickly. My excitement and anxiety mounted in the days before the retreat. As with any event, there were hurdles and questions that came up along the way. Since this was the first time I had ever organized this type of event, each hurdle made me very anxious until we landed on some resolution.

At one point, Ted's employer told him that he might not be able to take the scheduled time off in May. The fact that he might need to cancel with very little notice put us both in a tailspin. Especially since that potential issue wouldn't be resolved until the actual week of the event when he was cleared to attend…or told that he couldn't. I can't imagine how I would have gotten through the first retreat without someone else supporting the effort. Fortunately, Ted was cleared to attend and co-coordinate the retreat.

We also had a number of questions come up that made us have to establish foundational rules for both this retreat and any future events. Early on, I got an email from a woman whose husband knit. She wondered if MSKR was a gay event. I assured her that while the retreat would have gay men in attendance, it wasn't only for gay men, and that her husband was welcome to attend. I quickly realized she had a not-so-hidden agenda, when she responded that since the retreat was being held at a retreat center created by and for gay men and that the web page was hosted on QueerJoe.com, that she didn't feel comfortable sending her husband. My first reaction was to want to be snarky and sarcastic and respond with, "Perhaps you can understand how I feel at most events where I'm the only gay man." What I really wanted to ask, was if she was more concerned that her husband would be uncomfortable around gay men, or that he'd be way more comfortable than she was okay with. But I opted to go with a more charitable reply. I thanked her for her observations about the retreat and told her that I'd be glad to make him feel as comfortable as I could if he wanted to participate. I then purchased a new domain name, mensknittingretreat.com, to eliminate the one affiliation the retreat had to a queer blog.

This interaction helped me more fully realize the value of diversity in our communities. I highly encourage everyone to participate in an event where they are part of the minority…especially if they are usually in the majority. The experience might not be as comfortable, but it allows for the possibility of a vast amount of learning and a much more empathetic posture to others in the world.

We also had a trans man ask if he was welcome to attend. I had a definite opinion about this, but it seemed more and more that we were establishing what would be long-standing rules for future retreats. I opted to check Ted's thoughts before answering. In his uniquely simplistic way, he asked, "Is he a man?" I said yes. "Then he's welcome." It was no more complex than that.

One final example was an email from the wife of another guy-knitter. She wanted to attend with him as his spouse. She was infuriated that she was being excluded. I was glad Ted got to handle this response. He was glad that we had clearly thought through the rationale for why it was a retreat specifically for men. That it was in celebration of a community, rather than to be exclusionary. He was also pleased to be able to refer them to other co-ed knitting retreats where both of them could attend as a couple.

In the final weeks leading up to the retreat, I continued to execute the detailed project plan. I printed off personalized agendas and BINGO cards for each of the guys. I fortunately thought to print the attendee's three factoids on their own BINGO card, because many of the guys had forgotten completely what factoids they had provided to me. I also designed and printed a name tag for each guy that in addition to their name and the two logos for Easton Mountain and MSKR, also included their Ravelry ID and the profile photo they used on Ravelry. Since many of us only knew each other through Ravelry, we thought that their Ravelry profile photo would be a good way of helping us identify each other. Also, on the back of the name tag, I printed the attendee's abbreviated agenda to give them a quick reference to their schedule. We also printed signage and workshop rosters for all the volunteer workshop leaders.

There was a lot of informal communications to the guys attending via the Ravelry forum. You could tell the guys were very excited to be coming together. There was a lot of discussion about which projects to bring to work on, and which items they wanted to present at Show & Tell.

When the day finally arrived, I was on emotional overload. The car was packed with donated swag prizes, all the printed items, workshop materials for the workshop I offered to lead, and other items I thought might be useful. There was instant cocoa and microwave popcorn for movie night, as well as the DVD of the movie. We chose "Unconditional Love" with Kathy Bates and Rupert Everett because I thought it was lighthearted and fun, and it was a movie that had gone under the radar, so many of the guys had never seen it. I brought breathing nose-strips and ear-plugs to help reduce any issues of a snoring roommate. I also had the two five-pound boxes of M&Ms in the purple and green colors of the Easton Mountain logo and all the project bags and registration materials. I had also packed all my clothes and toiletries for the weekend and my own knitting projects. My car was surprisingly quite full.

This time, I had the full, printed, official directions to Easton Mountain. I still find it difficult to remember what it was like to find my way to places without GPS. I remember how much I hated having to print out MapQuest routes with detailed, turn-by-turn directions. But I did this time. I wasn't going to get lost on my second visit to Easton Mountain. It's about a four-hour drive from where I live to Easton Mountain, and I wasn't supposed to arrive until after 3:00 in the afternoon. But I still had to stop myself from leaving at 8:00 in the morning. I ended up leaving at 8:30. So, clearly I do have some willpower.

The number of years that I drove up to Schenectady New York made the drive to Upstate New York an easy task. It's one of those routes that my car seems to know how to navigate almost by itself. Only the last forty-five minutes of the drive were unfamiliar to me. The only thing I remember about my drive to Easton that day was the length of the dirt road that leads to Easton Mountain. It seemed shorter than the first time I visited. It was as if they had paved the road further than the last time I had been there. You'd have thought I'd be grateful for a longer section of paved road, but it only made me worry that I had missed a turn. So, you can imagine my relief when I saw the entry-road to Easton Mountain. I had thankfully arrived without incident. The driveway is an unpaved, rocky and rut-filled roadway, so I had to go somewhat slowly to make my way to the main lodge building at the end of the driveway, despite my inclination to race to get there. The view of the twin-peaked mountain and the pond brought a broad smile to my face.

As I parked my car, I saw Kenny, one of the guys registered for the retreat who had come up from the Washington, DC area. I recognized him from his Ravelry profile photo and on various knitting forums. I honestly think my exuberance in greeting him caught him off-guard and startled him a little bit. He got the brunt of all my built-up excitement as I greeted and hugged him. After months of anticipation, meeting Kenny made this whole venture a reality. It was actually happening.

We were both early, and Easton wasn't ready for us yet. We walked over to the Temple, a side building with a large porch and chatted while more and more guys arrived and joined us. Within an hour, we had a small group of exceedingly animated men. Some sitting and knitting, others actively engaged in interacting with the others. By the time 3:00 rolled around, we had a significant number of guys who had arrived. All of us were very eager to be part of the momentous group's coming-together.

The first official activity was dinner at 6:30. So when we were allowed to check in, many of us signed in with the front desk and got our room assignment. Ted and I were given a semi-private room together in the housing lodge. I unloaded the majority of my car in the main lodge building and the remainder of my clothes and toiletries in my assigned room. I returned right back to the great room to mingle and get to know everyone. I didn't want to miss one moment.

One of the aspects of Easton Mountain that I love is that gathering spaces do an amazing job of helping foster community. In the great room, there is living-room-like space, and a small nook they call the library with a few chairs surrounded by bookcases. The back deck is directly off the great room. There is a long porch facing the pond and the mountain directly outside the great room as well, and an enclosed area called the sun porch that also looks out over the pond and mountain. These are just the areas on the main floor of the lodge. On the floor below there are two small nooks where you can go off to be by yourself or have a one-on-one conversation with someone else. All these varied spaces allow for any options between being among a large, active group, to spending time in solitude and quiet.

Most of the guys coalesced in the great room for the first few hours. This is also where I set up the registration materials, like the small project bag, printed agendas and name tags.

It should be noted that from the very first moment, I felt nothing but love from each and every guy that I spent time with. But there were other indicators that this was going to be an exceptional group of guys. It may seem insignificant, but every one of the guys put on their name tag and kept it on throughout the event. This indicated to me that the guys were willing to be supportive and had respect for the other guys in the group. Perhaps I read more into the gesture, but minimally, it meant the guys weren't being deliberately antagonistic or trying to set themselves apart in any way.

The second phenomenon I noticed was how the guys interacted with each new guy as he arrived. They enthusiastically welcomed new arrivals into their smaller group and passed on any knowledge of what they had learned themselves so far. Where was the washroom? Was there a place to get water, coffee or tea? Who had the name tags. Each guy seemed to immediately take full responsibility for the welfare of everyone else. I honestly don't think I'd ever seen anything like this in any other group I'd ever been a part of.

While I had decided that as coordinator, it was my job to personally connect with every guy at the retreat and be consciously present with them during each interaction, it seemed like everyone was doing that as well. It was incredibly powerful. I had a bit of an advantage over the other guys in that I had been working with these names and information for months by the time I actually got to be with them. I knew where they lived, their Ravelry information and at least three facts about them.

Some of the guys knew each other prior to this event. There were other minor celebrities in the online knitting community who were popular and guys really wanted to meet them. There were a number of men from Canada. The weekend of the retreat fell on Victoria Day weekend in Canada, and Easton Mountain was a drivable distance for many places on their East coast. Most of the men were gay, but there were also a handful of straight guys as well. While I didn't know this, the first retreat had quite a few introverted men in attendance as well as many extroverted men. Being an extreme extrovert myself, I had a lot to learn about what it was like for an introvert at retreats like this, but that learning wouldn't come until subsequent years.

I also didn't realize at the time that in those first few hours, the full purpose of the retreat had already been realized. Without even having our first official activity, the guys had created a cohesive social fabric that was more stable than we could have possibly imagined. I remember stepping back for a moment to just observe and was more than thrilled to realize that each and every guy was fully engaged and participative with each other. This alone exceeded all expectations for me.

When dinner time came, we got the chance to meet the other retreat that was taking place at Easton Mountain the same weekend. Maturing Gay Men was a smaller group of guys with a program and materials created by a member, Ari Kane. This was at least his third year presenting the program at Easton Mountain. While their group would be holding their event in a different building on the property, there would be some activities, such as meals that would overlap.

The dinner bell rang and about forty guys plus the staff and volunteers at Easton Mountain grouped around the buffet island in the dining room. I hadn't realized that there was a custom of having a small prayer circle held before dinner each night. We all held hands and someone shared an impromptu blessing of thanks for the food, the staff and volunteers who had prepared it and the remainder of the community. My history with religious practice, including prayer, isn't a very positive one, so this unsettled me a bit. There were some of the other guys who were a bit put off by this unexpected spirituality as well. Ted, having been at Easton, knew of the custom and set an example for the rest of us. While he wasn't a religious person, he was open to participating in this small ritual of gratitude, and so most of us just politely followed suit.

Food at Easton Mountain is served buffet-style and was surprisingly good and quite generous. There were at least three selections for entrees including at least one vegetarian option and a host of sides, salads, bread and often soup. Once we filled our trays with food and drink, most of us took them into the sun porch area to sit with the others at long tables set up for communal eating. Given how much it looked like a school cafeteria, I had a fleeting concern that there would end up being a "cool kids" table or there would be some other evidence of exclusionary behavior. But that definitely didn't happen. Mostly the first guys to sit down took seats toward the back of the room because they were a bit more difficult to get to once the more forward seats were filled. So, again, the guys were all being supportive and considerate of the comfort and ease of the others.

Meals were also the primary time that Ted and I made announcements to the guys attending. This meal was the first time we addressed our fledgling group as a whole. We really only wanted to let the guys know how the next part of the retreat, the opening night circle, was an important part of the retreat and understanding how Easton Mountain functioned. Ted and I couldn't have been more thrilled that this event was underway and going extremely well.

Ted and I finished dinner and went to set up seating for the opening night circle. The Great Room is the main meeting space at Easton Mountain for groups our size. It is a spacious, sunny, 60' x 40' room with a wood-burning fireplace, hardwood floors, and large windows on three of the walls. Easton also provides padded floor chairs. I had never seen such a thing, but they're basically padded mats that bend in the center to form a chair so that people can sit comfortably on the floor, but they can also be stacked and put away when we're not meeting as a large group. Ted, Dave and I set up a circle of floor mats and readied ourselves for the official kick-off of the retreat.

For me, this was the moment that a full-fledged, amazing community cemented itself into existence. There was nothing exceptional that happened or that was said in those next two hours. But it became quite clear to everyone in the room that something very important had occurred, and they were an important part of it. This is the critical point of alchemy that has had me contemplating for years afterwards what exactly happened so that it could be reliably repeated each time.

Ted and I introduced ourselves and spoke briefly about how the retreat had come to be. We discussed the status of the retreat and that there were 32 guys in attendance. We went over all the logistics of workshops, the agenda, the project bag, the name tags, the housing assignments and where various amenities were on the property. We also discussed the fact that we were a diverse group. One of my favorite announcements we made that night was that there were straight men in the group, but we don't "out" anyone, so they could feel free to do that themselves if they wanted.

Dave, our Easton Mountain liaison and co-participant in the retreat went over a litany of facts, rules and important information about Easton Mountain. Then we took questions.

As I noted, there was nothing extraordinary, and yet something extraordinary took place. Some critical mass of joy, support and love had taken place that carried our group to an experience that was transformative.

In the glow of this newfound experience, we released the guys to play Get To Know You BINGO. Their interactions for this activity and for the remainder of the retreat were engaged, supportive and joyous. Kenny ended up getting BINGO incredibly quickly and getting first choice in swag prizes.

All that I remember for the remainder of that night is that I didn't want to miss anything. Some of the guys had a long travel day and went to bed early. Others opted to head up to Easton Mountain's beautiful wood-burning sauna or downstairs to soak in the hot tub. Me, I stayed around the great room until everyone else had gone to bed and then headed to my room as well. I wanted to absorb every bit of this experience as I could. I also felt some level of obligation to be around in case anyone needed something on their first night.

The following morning, the bird-song around the housing lodge was extremely loud and it helped me get up rather early. I went down to the main lodge building and participated in yoga with the resident yogi and massage therapist, Tim. I don't usually do yoga, and even the gentle, beginner yoga that Tim presented to a small group of guys made me huff and puff more than I would have expected. But it seemed an apt way of waking up at Easton Mountain, and I was glad for the movement and meditative serenity it offered me.

I went in search of coffee. One of the small things that I love about Easton is that some of the volunteers and staff get up early and start coffee each morning. There is coffee, tea and water available all day. I wasn't the first one down to the main building, so I sat, drank coffee and greeted anyone coming down to start their day. The familiarity we had established with each other from the previous night was remarkable. The guys were eager to be back in communion on the Saturday morning of the retreat. There had been some smaller groups and couples who had bonded, but even the newfound cliques weren't exclusive. They welcomed others to join as well.

I finally squeezed in a bit of time to call home and check in and then take a shower and dress for the day. Then back to the lodge for breakfast and announcements.

As with any event, there were some issues. Uncomfortable beds, snoring roommates, difficulty sleeping in a new environment, low water pressure, etc. One of the biggest complaints was the smell of the water. This is not a new thing for Easton Mountain. Greenwich, NY is near Saratoga Springs, and as I like to say, Easton Mountain rests on the same delicate aquifer as the spas that sprung up years ago in Saratoga Springs to take advantage of the medicinal properties of the water. The water is high in sulfur and smells like it. Depending on how high the water table is will affect how much medicinal aroma is in the water. Surprisingly, the water has no apparent healing properties, but fortunately, it also has no detrimental effects either except for the times when the smell is strong.

Back in 2008, I was the type of person who didn't do well with multiple, overlapping emotions. Especially when there are conflicting emotions going on concurrently. I preferred my emotions to come in one at a time, pure and simple…even if it's grief, anger or any of the "bad" emotions. But this first morning of the retreat, I was having at least five different emotions. I was still feeling fear and anxiety that the entire event would fall apart. Then there was joy and love in the afterglow of the previous night. I also felt a lot of excitement and anticipation for what would happen in the upcoming day. Finally, there was also a very deep sense of safety and serenity that I had difficulty reconciling with all the other things going on. I didn't really have the luxury of sitting down and examining any of these feelings even if I'd had the capacity to sort through them all.

For me, the result of having a slew of emotions is often the experience of being overwhelmed.

At one point during Saturday morning, the sense of being overwhelmed took over. I don't recall what prompted it. Perhaps one of the guys expressed some concern about something, or one of the staff alerted me to a new problem. But whatever it was, it tipped the scales and put me into full overwhelmed mode. I stood in a crowded great room feeling panicky and anxious and at a loss as to what to do. While the situation felt huge to me, I doubt that many of the guys even noticed I was having a moment. But at least one of them did. One of the guys, Jeff, who I had never met until the previous day crossed the great room walking directly toward me and as he came up beside me put his arm around my shoulder and gently guided me toward the library nook of the room where it was a little less bustling. He leaned down and calmly said to me, "Remember, it's just knitting." Then he smiled reassuringly and said, "How can I help?"

Well, you can imagine how much he had already helped. The one simple, supportive statement had the immediate effect of putting everything into perspective and my anxiety had vanished. His one simple question made me realize that I was fully supported and every guy in attendance wanted only for this event to be amazing.

Whatever it was that put me into a tailspin was quickly figured out and I was clear-eyed and fully present as we went into the next portions of the retreat.

That day we had scheduled workshops and a road trip to a local alpaca farm. It all went extremely smoothly. All of the activities we had scheduled were simply to put a structure around the formation of a community. This wasn't a conscious decision, but I think Ted and I understood innately that any activities we added to the retreat were mainly to support bringing the guys together in a deeply connected way. Even getting to pet a newly born alpaca on our roadtrip was just window-dressing that helped bring us together in a shared, beautiful experience.

There was surprisingly very little coordination that needed to be done during the retreat. Ted and I worked well together announcing the times when various workshops began. Meals were always a good time to communicate to the full group. but for the most part, the retreat progressed with very little guidance from the leaders. It seems as though all the pre-retreat preparations and setting a clear agenda, made for a relatively effortless event.

I took the opportunity to make sure that I connected with each of the guys personally. In addition to getting to know these guys, I also wanted them to feel acknowledged and seen as a critical member of the group. I knew some of the guys through their participation in online forums, blogs and podcasts. Other guys, like Jeff, I didn't even know how they knew about the retreat.

Jeff, Steve and Scott were three of the guys I didn't know at all prior to the retreat. Turns out that they had all recently attended a LGBTQ camp called Camp Camp. One of the activities at the event was a knitting workshop that the three guys had attended and Jeff had learned to knit there. When one of them found out about the Men's Knitting Retreat, he decided it would be a great place to reunite. These three guys had an immense talent for fostering community and knew the kinds of friendships that could be established in an environment like the retreat. I was really glad they brought that sense of connection to the MSKR that first year.

While I won't be able to go through the entire roster of the 32 men who attended that first retreat, I will specifically mention one other man. Stephen came in from San Francisco for the retreat. He and a friend (who did not come to the retreat) were doing one of the earlier podcasts back then called Y-Knit. It was a podcast specifically about the men's knitting community, in that the "Y" in Y-Knit was referring to the male or Y chromosome. Stephen is smart and funny and quirky in a really delightful way. Most of the guys fully enjoyed interacting with him. In part, he came to the retreat to record an interview with Ted and I for the podcast. But like most of us, he was blown away by the amazing community of the retreat. I think it was the very essence of what he and his podcast partner were trying to examine in their podcast. He did interview me and Ted and created a podcast episode about the retreat, but his experience of the retreat went much deeper than that, especially when it came to the expansion of this group to help initiate other retreats.

One of the other traditions that began at the first event was the Show & Tell night. It was scheduled after dinner on Saturday. The basic premise of Show & Tell is to give the guys an opportunity to show off any yarn project they've completed. We basically set up all the floor-seats in a circle as we had for the first night. Similar to a fashion show runway, guys are encouraged to show off any items that they knitted, crocheted, spun, wove, etc. Ted and I had agreed that it was also to show very public praise and encouragement to a group that might not get enough of it in their other knitting communities.

A pleasant and surprising event that occurred, was a request we got from the Maturing Gay Men group. Up until that point in the retreat, the guys attending the other event going on at Easton Mountain that weekend were very much doing their own event, completely independent of our group. They were in a different space on the property and they were even housed in rooms with each other, so we had very little interaction with them except as noted previously, at meals. They somehow caught wind of the fact that we were going to have a Show & Tell. They asked if they could attend as part of the audience. Some of the staff and volunteers at Easton also made the same request. Honestly, it surprised both Ted and me that others would be interested in our art-craft.

The Show & Tell turned out to be enormously successful. The guys' experience-level with yarn crafts varied from very beginner to highly advanced. There were some truly astounding pieces that were displayed that night which got a lot of very well-deserved praise from the others. But even the less experienced guys who presented their projects got tons of praise and encouragement. It was clear that everyone was fully behind making sure everyone received plentiful accolades for their efforts. The bonus surprise was the reaction from the non-knitters. They were blown away. I'm not sure what they expected, but the talent they evidenced seemed to far exceed any ideas of what they thought our members were able to do.

After the uplifting experience of the Show & Tell, we finished off the Saturday of the retreat with a slumber party/movie night to let the guys relax and get even more comfortable with each other. As with most of the other nights, there were some of the guys that drifted up to their rooms to sleep, others who took advantage of the wood-burning sauna, and others like me, who stayed up until the last guys went to bed. We didn't want to miss one second of the event.

The following day, Sunday, would be the final day of the retreat, ending after lunch. We had a time slot in the agenda for the final workshops of the retreat, and then a live feedback session. We didn't quite understand just how important the feedback session would be. One of things we really wanted to know is if the guys would be interested in making this an annual event. Resoundingly, they did. Instead of just providing feedback on what worked and what didn't, they wanted to actively participate in directing what the retreat should look like going forward. It basically turned into a planning session for the following year. Mostly, they wanted a longer event. It was clear that three days and two nights was not enough time to revel with this incredible community. Other than that, there weren't any significant changes they wanted to make to the retreat.

Dave, Ted and I had achieved even more than we had hoped and sparked something that had the potential for having a long-term impact on the men's fiber-arts community. My only remaining concern was that this event might be one of those times where its brightness would burn it out too quickly. That there would be a crash and burn after the event that would negate all that had happened. There were two examples in my life of this kind of overexcitement followed by a crash - Christmas and school plays. As a child, the excitement and anticipation of Christmas was always stoked by my parents and siblings. For weeks and weeks I'd yearn for Christmas morning and like millions of other families who celebrate Christmas, it would be over in a frenzied millisecond and the crash was always immediate. The sense of, "Is that all there is?" was almost debilitating. Similarly, participating in high school drama had a similar effect. The euphoria of being cast in a show and the build-up of rehearsals, stage building, costumes, props and blocking. All of this building to an exhilarating opening night and celebratory cast party after closing night. Then…nothing. It was always painful the first week after a show for me. No rehearsals, no anticipation, just what felt like an abyss.

All the components leading up to the retreat had the same components of anticipation and joyous exuberance for all the attendees. Like Christmas, we encouraged the enthusiasm and excitement months before the event occurred. But there was no crash for me after this event. Somehow, the deep connection of community that occurred was not short-lived. The joy of coming together as a group seemed to create a fabric that was stable and the joy persisted instead of unraveling. Not only did the deep satisfaction of the event continue, it actually grew.

There were a number of follow-up communications with the guys. Easton Mountain sent out a list of attendees with names, addresses, email addresses and photos so that we could stay in-touch. We solicited any additional feedback that the guys had either forgotten to mention or preferred to mention in a less public way. There was much sharing about this quite extraordinary event on various knitting forums and blogs and podcasts. It was officially a phenomenon and by group dictate, it became an annually scheduled event.

Chapter 14
The Idiot-Cord of Communities

"Passion makes idiots of the cleverest men, and makes the biggest idiots clever."

Francois de La Rochefoucauld

There is a technique in knitting called the i-cord. The "i" allegedly is short for idiot, in that this technique is pretty much idiot-proof. It's strikingly similar to the tubular fabric that first sparked my interest in knitting, except it only has a few stitches in the tube. It creates a very thin tube, or a cord. If you've ever seen an empty, wooden thread-spool with four nails in the top and yarn-cord going down the center of the spool, you've seen i-cord.

After the thrill and exhilaration of the first Men's Knitting Retreat, I started to think that the success of the first retreat was less about what we had done than it was an inevitability - that we were the i-cord of communities and that any similar group of fiber-loving guys who got together would have an equally profound experience of being together. Perhaps the 2008 MSKR already had the success built in and that we just happened to chance on the right combination of factors for it to burst into reality.

Ted and I both hoped we'd had some impact on the success of the event other than just gathering a group of guys at a retreat center. But perhaps the event was idiot-proof and we were just the fortunate idiots. The questions started rising up in my head. Was this just a simple chain-reaction of events that was random and would have eventually happened if Ted and I hadn't ever met? Or did the careful curating of an environment and a space for creating community by Ted and I create this vibrant community? We were receptive to all the questions that came up. They gave us a chance to experiment and try out new methods over the subsequent years to see which components of a retreat worked well and which weren't as successful.

I-cord is a somewhat derogatory misnomer for the cord-producing, knitting technique. It isn't really idiot-proof. Not only does it require some knowledge and skill to make i-cord, but it also teaches some valuable lessons about creating a stable knitted fabric that can be used even by very advanced knitters. Ted and I suspected that our knowledge and skills at building community added a necessary ingredient. We were pretty certain that the first retreat was not idiot-proof. We also hoped that our first surprisingly successful attempt at building a stable community would provide us valuable lessons for re-creating the community going forward.

Chapter 15
A Completed Gauge Swatch

"The purpose of knitting a swatch is not to match gauge, it's to make a fabric you like and to know its gauge."

Patty Lyons

I've learned that when I begin a new knitting design, the first rows of fabric do not necessarily foretell how successful the project will be. It requires at least four inches of fabric to know for certain that the yarn and the stitch pattern are going to work and that the fabric will be suitable for the purposes of the intended garment. Many knitters make a gauge swatch before embarking on a full garment. The gauge swatch is used for a number of different purposes. Primarily, if you're following a pattern, and you want your garment to come out to the correct final size, it's necessary to measure your stitches per inch, or your gauge, to make sure you're creating the same size fabric as the pattern designer. But it's also useful for assessing if the yarn works well with the stitch pattern and if the drape of the knitted fabric is what you're looking to create. Some of the less risk-averse knitters will forgo a test swatch and just jump right into a project, knowing that they might need to rip back and re-knit the beginnings of the garment. Others, like me, have a very fluid definition of a gauge swatch. Often, when making a garment like a sweater, I start with a sleeve, and call that my swatch. This first Men's Knitting Retreat felt a bit like jumping in without a swatch at all.

Ted, Dave and I were overjoyed with how well the retreat had gone. At every step along the way it had exceeded, and often far exceeded what we thought was possible. The number of attendees, the caliber of guys, the diversity in geographic location, the distance each guy was willing to travel, and most definitely, the capacity to coalesce. In that last aspect, our expectations were most definitely far exceeded. The initial gauge swatch was a clear success.

There was an immediate and unexpected response to the event and all the attention it received afterwards. Stephen, our San Francisco-based attendee, went home and told his podcast partner, Michael about the retreat. He told him that they had to do something like MSKR on the West Coast. Michael hadn't attended MSKR, but Stephen's excitement was contagious. Michael completely understood the possibilities and got extremely excited about having their own event on the West Coast.

I knew Michael only virtually through his blog and podcast, and knitting forums. Up until that point, we had never met in-person. It turns out that he's like me in many ways - at least in that he pursued putting together the new retreat with an enormous amount of enthusiasm, energy and excitement. He organized the first Men's Fall Knitting Retreat (MFKR) in a matter of months.

Friday, November 7, 2008, Michael hosted the first West Coast Men's Knitting Retreat in Sausalito, California. It took place at a YMCA conference center in a venue on the bluffs between the Pacific Ocean and the San Francisco Bay, called Point Bonita. Nineteen guys attended that retreat, including Ted, Stephen and Kenny from the east coast retreat.

The MFKR was modeled after the east coast retreat, although it had its own, distinct vibe. Michael had a lot of contacts with larger fiber vendors, so he was able to solicit a lot of donations as prizes for the guys. In fact, one of the men who attended the west coast retreat worked for a large importer of knitting needles and yarns in the Seattle area, who donated project bags for each of the attendees. So, Michael didn't have to go scrounging through dollar stores for a proper bag to give the guys when they arrived. Michael also liked the structure in place at the east coast retreat, so he used a similar agenda, with workshops and a Show & Tell. I wasn't able to attend the first west coast retreat, and I was envious of missing out on the creation of community and the exuberance that comes along with it. Like the men on the east coast, the guys on the west coast were overjoyed with the event. They definitely got to experience the same excitement of transformation we had experienced a few months earlier.

The east coast event could have been seen as our test-sleeve-swatch, in that it demonstrated that we could successfully build a vibrant and wondrous community. The west coast retreat was the event that showed the experience could be replicated. There seemed to be an even larger demand for us to replicate the experience of forming this community. It was looking like this fabric of community was going to work out fantastically well. The only question remaining for me was whether the community would persist and grow. Was the fabric stable enough for the overall garment as it grew in size and scope?

It looked like we were going to need a bit more structure to support these two retreats and any future events that might emerge. Minimally we needed a web site and better logo than I had been able to throw together. Franklin stepped in and designed our first official logo that replaced my rudimentary image of a skein of yarn and needles. I also purchased the domain name mensknittingretreat.com to establish our space on the internet. We started to document the past retreats and set up a space to promote upcoming retreats. We also put together a document on how to create your own Men's Knitting Retreat. Most importantly, we documented the three foundational ideas that defined what we considered to be a Men's Knitting Retreat. First, it had to be for men as a way of celebrating the men's knitting community. Second, it should be not-for-profit and hopefully not-for-loss either. Finally, we highly recommended that no outside talent should be brought in to teach or facilitate the retreat - volunteers should be solicited to coordinate, organize and facilitate the event and any workshops. Having as much of the effort that goes into a retreat being done by members from within our own ranks, made it a lot more organic and allowed us to focus more on what we considered our primary goal. To foster and celebrate this fantastic community. It also made the events more affordable so that more guys would be able to attend. Each of the efforts of setting up an organizational structure to support the retreats made the community more solid and real. It cemented the experience in a way that made it feel stable and reliable.

Fewer than fifty guys had gotten to experience the magic of the two retreats in May and November of 2008, but it seemed as though the excitement had reached some level of critical mass in the men's knitting community. There were discussions on blogs, podcasts and in knitting forums. The buzz was starting to get loud. It was clear that the experience of the retreat was something meaningful and important for those who had experienced it.

Ted and I began organizing the second MSKR for May of 2009. We found that the Victoria Day weekend in Canada worked well for both the Canadians and the guys from the States. It's always the weekend before Memorial Day weekend in the States, so it's not a busy travel weekend for many of us. It's also not a peak weekend for Easton Mountain. Based on the feedback from the first event, we expanded the retreat to four days and three nights. We also decided to rent out the full retreat center from Easton Mountain and conduct our own registration. This required that we contract and pay for a minimum of 40 guys. The only other change we made was calculating a registration fee that would allow us some budget for expenses. We made a gamble that there would be at least 40 guys who wanted to attend the retreat.

At about the same time, we had two additional requests for regional retreats. James, a knitter and yarn store owner from New Zealand who had attended the west coast retreat, decided he wanted to organize a retreat in New Zealand. He blocked out rooms at a retreat center in Wellington and scheduled the first international, four-day/three-night Men's Knitting Retreat for March of 2009.

Across the globe, Todd, who hadn't attended either of the two first retreats, asked how he could organize a Midwest

Men's Knitting Retreat in Michigan to take place in November of 2009. He reserved a space at a retreat/campground in Delton, Michigan.

Finally, Michael had already begun scheduling the second west coast retreat. Based on feedback from the first event, he decided to move the event to the Seattle area, and chose a beautiful setting, on a bluff overlooking Puget Sound called Dumas Bay Centre.

We now had four Men's Knitting Retreats scheduled for 2009. If the number of messages and emails asking about the retreat was any indication, the number of very interested men was going to increase quickly. The in-person retreats had really animated the men's knitting community and more and more guys knew they wanted to take part in these extraordinary events. Without exception, the guys who wrote about the retreats had difficulty expressing the full experience. It was clear that the coming-together of these two small groups of guys had sparked something unexpected and wonderful. It quickly became obvious that the transformative nature of the retreats was a common experience shared by all the guys who attended.

Now we had to see if it was sustainable. Could we repeat the joyous transformation on an annual basis with different groups of guys? My suspicion was that we could, but on some of my less positive days, the doubts would creep in. I mean really…how could we have that kind of miracle happen twice?

James brought together eight guys from California, Australia and of course, New Zealand for the New Zealand

Men's Knitting Retreat. Even in a smaller sized group, the guys enjoyed both establishing a new and vibrant community as well as participating in a local community that was affiliated with a larger group.

For me and Ted, the approach of the May 2009 retreat came with the same amount of anxiety and worry. They were just different anxieties and worries. I didn't have to worry about the structure, or the general guidelines of the retreat, thanks to the structure Ted and Dave and I had put in place on the first retreat. I didn't have to be concerned about so many unknowns as I had the first year. The anxieties of the second year were that the bar had been set very high. The general buzz in the online men's knitting community created a level of expectation in the potential attendees that was definitely worrisome for me. I really needed Jeff to reach out and remind me again that it's just knitting.

We were able to register 40 guys for the retreat without difficulty. We ended up opening it up to a total of 42 guys for the May, 2009 retreat. About three quarters of the guys from 2008 registered to return for the second MSKR in 2009. The returning group was definitely a sufficient critical mass of those who experienced the magic of the first year to help convey that to the new guys. I recall stepping back after the initial opening circle as I had the first year, and realizing that each and every guy was again enthusiastically engaged in helping form this most amazing fabric of community.

The four-day (Thursday - Sunday) Labor Day weekend became firmly established as the timeframe for the Men's

Fall Knitting Retreat taking place near Seattle, Washington. I did end up attending the second MFKR in 2009 with 27 other guys. It was hosted by Mike again and I was joined by Jeff, Kenny, James (from New Zealand), Stephen (from San Francisco) and Franklin. The venue was an old convent overlooking the Puget Sound. Rooming and dining were just perfect and the meeting space was ideal with big windows overlooking the grounds and waters of the Sound. Mike continued with the standard format and agenda for the retreat which included workshops volunteered by the guys attending, Show & Tell and a visit to a warehouse of yarn, knitting needles and any other notions a guy like me might want to purchase. Having a participant role at this retreat allowed me to see the dynamics of the retreat from a slightly different perspective. It was incredibly gratifying that these events reliably continued to attract an extraordinary group of guys.

A dozen guys also went to the first Midwest Men's Knitting Retreat in November of 2009. Their agenda included a roadtrip to a local sheep farm. The organizer Todd was a knitwear designer whose pattern I had used to knit an early sweater for the sister-out-of-law. He was able to bring together an array of guys from Chicago, Michigan and Northwestern New York. That first Michigan retreat included a relatively new knitter, Stephen West who would eventually become one of the most popular knitwear designers for hand knitters. Like Franklin, he has become our version of an A-list knitting celebrity. These guys seemed to very quickly form a loyalty to what would eventually become the Great Lakes Men's Knitting Retreat. When Todd opted not to volunteer to coordinate the retreat the following year, one of the prior year's participants, Barry, stepped in and continued the annual event.

Chapter 16
Retreating

"Nowhere can man find a quieter or more untroubled retreat than his own soul."

Marcus Aurelius

The commonality that brings men together at these events is their love of fiber-crafts. The workshops, roadtrips and the Show & Tell all focus on fiber-crafts. When we combine the commonality of the group, with the opportunity to retreat from daily life, and the beauty and serenity of the venues for the retreats, the guys take the opportunity to create the most beautiful tapestry of community. It's as if the structure of the retreat is simply a plying together of a beautiful yarn and the guys intuitively know how to transform this yarn into an extraordinary fabric.

Ted came up with the name, Men's Knitting Retreat. I'm not sure if he gave much thought to the word "retreat" when he came up with the title. It could just as easily have been called Men's Knitting Camp, Men's Yarn-Craft Conference, Men's Fiber Escape or a multitude of other titles indicating that a group of guys who participated in fiber-craft were going to join together at a designated place at a specified date and time.

Knowing Ted, the word retreat was most likely a deliberate and conscious decision. Whenever we had questions of what was the purpose of our event, reminding ourselves of the definition of the word "retreat" often helped us to arrive at an answer that was consistent with the intent of the events.

All of the regional retreats take place in venues that are more off the beaten path and secluded. The beauty of nature at these locations plays an important part in setting the tone for the event. The retreats are also multiple night events where you are housed and fed at the retreat. Both of these components support the idea of retreating from day-to-day tasks of life. Ted and I intended for the guys to leave behind their work, errands, worries and anything else that might distract them. Further, we tried to create an environment that best supported the men coming together in ways that are impactful and sometimes even life-changing.

In addition to the natural beauty of the location, and providing for their basic needs, we also try to create a space where the men can retreat from the worries of having to meet obligations of societal pressures. In a space of acceptance, everyone there can relax and enjoy being simply who they are. The result is an amazing environment where strong relationships and deep connectedness is possible.

At the first event, the environment that allowed for the guys to retreat had to be created and modeled so that the first 32 guys could truly retreat and enjoy themselves. Once we had a core group of guys who continued to return for subsequent retreats, there was already built-in support for creating the space from the previous attendees. They have made it incredibly easy to carry forward the environment for re-creating miraculous events over and over.

During the years that the Men's Knitting Retreats were growing, Franklin Habit had become one of the A-list celebrities in the knitting world. Through his blog, his alter-ego cartoon sheep, Dolores, a published book of his cartoons, and his alliance with some of the larger commercial yarn vendors, he had garnered much well-earned attention. He had also developed a portfolio of knitting workshops on various techniques that always sold out immediately at the various knitting conventions. During a conversation with him, I was urging him to attend the next Men's Spring Knitting Retreat. Given that knitting had become his profession, he was concerned it would be like work for him - that it would require that he be "on" with the other guys. When I described our concept of retreating, he immediately saw the possibilities.

He decided to register and as an attendee, he did get to retreat from his role as a knit-workshop instructor and establish some profoundly connected relationships with the other guys. He went even further to actually volunteer to lead fiber-related workshops at the retreat. When it was clear he could do it for the joy of contributing to the retreat community, he was pleased to offer. It was incredibly gratifying to provide Franklin a knitting space where he could unwind and be his authentic self and not feel compelled to be a particular way as he might in front of the knitting community at large. Even more gratifying was knowing that the same safe, laid-back space was available for everyone who comes to the retreats.

One of the benefits of the retreat-able space was that the coordinators get to participate in it and take advantage of the benefits as well. In my dealings with all of the regional coordinators over the years, they have always expressed how satisfying it is to participate in the community both as a member and as a facilitator. This is largely the reason that all of the retreats are organized and facilitated by volunteers who eagerly pursued being the regional coordinator in their local area.

As with all the regional coordinators, I get to retreat from my day-to-day life even at the retreats where I am the coordinator. I also get to establish meaningful connections with the guys who are there. Yes, I continue to get heaps of praise for all that I do to make the retreats happen, and I'm grateful for the accolades. But if the work I do to put together an event ever got to the point where it wasn't completely joyous and satisfying, no amount of praise would keep me doing it. I make it clear to anyone who thanks me for my work on the retreats, that it is a complete joy to do and I am immensely grateful for the opportunity. Even more so, I get to be deeply involved in the community months before the actual retreat. Setting up the web site for registration, opening registration, maintaining the master list of attendees, communicating to all the attendees and working on all the parts of the retreat keeps me involved in a very joyous way. Project bags, giveaways, name tags, agendas, workshop materials - all of these tasks let me involve myself with all the guys for months before we ever gather. The guys get to anticipate the event, and I get to both prepare the space and anticipate at the same time. It never feels less than a complete blessing to get to do both.

After every one of the retreats that I have been to, I find myself satisfied and joyful for weeks afterwards. For some reason, it seems as though the magic of weaving a community leaves me fulfilled...filled up in a way that is energizing and satisfying for long after the event. I'm not sure why this is. The only explanation I've come up with is that the joy of being with one's people is different from other highly-anticipated events.

Chapter 17
The Durability of Our Knitted Community

*"Success is not the absence of failure; it's
the persistence through failure."*

Aisha Tyler

When knitting a functional garment, durability can be an important aspect to the fabric that makes up the garment. Especially when the garment is put under some stress. Similarly, our community needed to be able to withstand some difficulties as well.

In 2019, Barry, who had jumped in to carry on the Great Lakes Men's Knitting Retreat into its second year, passed away. He had coordinated the retreat for nine years and had established many recurring customs each year for the loyal group of guys who attended, including his wife making her famous lasagna for the guys on the first unofficial meal of the retreat. Stephen, one of the local attendees at the retreat, volunteered to take over the helm, keeping in place much of what Barry had established. The local group was incredibly strong and continues to fully support whoever is facilitating this group that is so important to them.

Then in November of 2022, Ted, the founding father of the Men's Knitting Retreats died unexpectedly. From a functional perspective, Ted had stopped coordinating the MSKR in 2012, so there was no disruption in our ability to continue the Easton Mountain Retreat. But we lost the opportunity to seek his counsel and the stability of his ongoing support. Again, it was a huge loss to our community, but the guys came together and helped carry forward Ted's legacy.

Another test of our durability came in early March of 2020. Plans were well underway to host the thirteenth Men's Spring Knitting Retreat at Easton Mountain. We had 43 guys registered. Registration had filled up in the first two days after it opened at the beginning of January. We also had a finalized agenda of workshops that had been volunteered by the participants and the guys were getting more and more excited about the approach of May. I had sent the second deposit to Easton Mountain at the beginning of March and plans were moving along smoothly.

On March 3rd, Thaddeus read an article about a virus that had made its way to the States. Unlike me, he knew immediately that it was going to be something we needed to prepare for. He insisted that we go to our warehouse store, and stock up on canned goods. He was convinced that there was a strong chance that we would be confined to our house and we should have at least a month of supplies to allow us to be isolated in our house. Thaddeus wasn't usually so alarmist, and honestly, I was dubious. I thought he was totally overreacting. My perspective was reinforced when we went shopping the next day and it wasn't overly crowded. The populace wasn't in a panic about this new virus. As we were checking out, I casually mentioned why we had so many canned goods to the cashier and a customer next to me grumbled under her breath that we were just fear-mongering. I silently agreed with her, but figured we'd eventually use all this food or donate it to a local food bank.

It was only a matter of days when Thaddeus' worries became a reality. The novel coronavirus, soon to be known as COVID-19 was becoming a full-fledged pandemic and the possibility of having everything shut down was becoming more and more real. Despite the panicked purchasing of hand sanitizer, face masks and paper goods at every grocery store across the country, it still took me at least another week to get past my denial and realize we would need to cancel the retreat. Within a few weeks, it would have been out of my hands anyway, as the Mayor of New York State was closing down any public gatherings for the foreseeable future. I was shocked and heartsick at the loss.

There was much to do to stop the forward motion of the retreat, and I didn't want to do any of it. The immediacy of deciding refund and cancellation protocols, negotiating with the retreat center and drafting communications, demanded that I get ultra-organized and power through it all. Fortunately, many of the tasks allowed me to interact with a group of guys I had come to love. I had to keep reminding myself that these guys were mourning the loss of the community as well and it was that exact mourning that reminded me that they valued the community as much as I did.

There was another overwhelming concern lurking in the back of my mind, which I was able to leave uninvestigated with all the immediate busy-ness of canceling the retreat. Would this community be able to withstand what looked like possibly a two-year break and still be able to re-form when (if) we were able to get together in May of 2022? Would there be a sufficient critical mass of community-memory of the regular attendees to pass down to any new members of the group? I had to trust that there would be and also remind myself that we had successfully created this amazing space in the past. I was certain we could do it again.

We also looked at any virtual alternatives we had. Zoom was starting to become the go-to software for video-conferencing, so we scheduled a virtual drop-in session on May 16th, which was the scheduled Saturday of the retreat. It was well attended, but there was an overall tone of sadness and mourning that we couldn't be together in-person.

Doug, one of the regular attendees of the retreat had moved to Palm Springs and had set up two weekly, in-person meet-ups with local knitters prior to the onset of COVID. One was co-ed and the other was a men's fiber group meet-up. When they were interrupted by the pandemic, they set up virtual meetings via Zoom for the two events each week. The Zoom sessions were only open to those who had already been members of the group prior to lockdown. Doug quickly gained an understanding of how to best use video-conferencing and how to virtually hold the space of a meeting in such a way that a community could form in the absence of physical proximity.

I was sorely missing the Men's Knitting Retreat community and I also wanted to see if I could bridge the gap between the times when we all could be together in-person. I decided to set up a daily 3-hour virtual videoconference for any men who were into fiber arts. Every day, from 12:30 to 3:30, I hosted a videoconference and announced it on various online men's fiber forums. The daily sessions never fully replicated the intensity of the retreats, but they definitely satisfied my desire to be with my people. I also wouldn't have guessed it, but these daily videoconferences end up continuing for over two years. It was a very different experiment than the retreats and an equally different community experience. With Doug's help, I had to learn a new set of facilitation skills to help foster community virtually. We had a significant number of guys attend on a regular basis and there were also a number of guys who showed up every once in a while. The core community of regulars were a mix of guys I knew from the retreats and others I got to know only as part of the daily videoconferences.

There were two unexpected experiences that happened with the virtual get-togethers that helped me understand the components of a structurally sound community-fabric.

The first was that many of the new guys to our virtual group often had a great need to express themselves. It happened repeatedly that a new person would come into the group and would take over the conversation with a constant stream of talking. The first few times this happened, I just thought the new members were being selfish and impolite. They seemed to not be able to read the room and their interactions appeared overbearing. But eventually, their monologue would wind down and the newcomer would start to interact with everyone else with more ease and social finesse. I realized that these guys weren't being purposefully rude. They were in a state of social deprivation as a result of the isolation of the pandemic. They needed to express a backlog of thoughts and feelings and ideas. In most cases, the established group members just let the new guys express themselves as much as they needed and the situation usually resolved itself.

The second situation was the inevitable problem of people with varying opinions on controversial issues who wanted to discuss them in a group setting. Usually these guys had a specific agenda and felt it was their responsibility to sway opinions to the "correct" side of the controversial issue. The Palm Springs virtual groups came up with a great solution. During one of their weekly, virtual meetups, the controversial topic of putting pineapple on pizza came up. As you can imagine, the conversation got heated. Finally, Doug as the group administrator had to step in and squelch the topic. From then on, whenever anyone was feeling uncomfortable with a topic, they could call "pineapple pizza." The new group rule stated that anytime anyone called a pineapple pizza, the topic being discussed had to change immediately. In the various men's virtual meet-ups, the pineapple pizza rule became commonly understood. It turned out to be a very fair and democratic way to keep controversy out of the meetings without any individual guy feeling as though they were being singled out and censored.

The pandemic created a few other obstacles over the next few years as well. We eventually ended up having the NorthEast Men's Fall retreat in September of 2020. A brief window opened where new COVID cases were low enough to relax the limits on gatherings in New York State. Both to comply with the retreat center's requirement and for our own safety, we needed to put in place vaccine tracking and pre-retreat testing for all the attendees. The introduction of the vaccines in late 2020 allowed for many of us to get vaccinated and make it through the 10-day post-vaccine window in time to attend the 2021 Men's Spring Knitting Retreat. It was a much smaller group that year with only 25 guys in attendance which made both social distancing and getting to spend time with each of the guys much easier.

My initial worries about withstanding the break in community turned out to be unfounded. We picked up right where we had left it with a bond between us that was strong and vibrant. In some ways, the bond was even sturdier because we had had an opportunity to realize just how much we were missing when we weren't able to get together. Summarizing these few years for myself was analogous to finding my favorite hand-knit socks with moth holes in the ankle section of the sock. While you may have been able to adequately darn and fix the holes and make the socks wearable, the evidence of damage is still there. At the same time, the comfort and joy of wearing these socks was definitely worth the effort of repair.

Our exceptional community had successfully withstood hardship and proved itself capable of making it through the pause in getting together. Yes, it left a mark on our history that many of us will still be reminded of. But it also gave many of us the understanding of just how important this community and these retreats are in our lives. Having risked losing the retreats, made them all that much more valued in our lives.

Chapter 18
An Assessment of The Fabric We Made

"The trouble with most of us is that we would rather be ruined by praise than saved by criticism."

Norman Vincent Peale

Providing my younger-knitter-self with feedback on my first sweater was a useful exercise. It demonstrated the kind of progress I had made since. I originally started knitting. The regional coordinators of the various Men's Knitting Retreats are similarly looking back at their events and assessing their successes and shortfalls in how they are able to create the fabric of community. Most of us end each retreat by asking the guys in attendance if they want to have another retreat in the following year. And if they do, what we can do to make it more meaningful, enjoyable or worthwhile for them. What aspects of the retreat do they want continued and what aspects would they like to see improved. It's not always easy for a group who has learned to be encouraging and supportive of each other to critique an event. But fortunately, we have a longstanding history now of being receptive to their comments. So many of the guys who have been to multiple retreats will start us off with helpful comments to demonstrate how even criticism can be supportive and useful.

Whenever I am asked to assess someone else's knitting, I try to straddle the line between being encouraging and also providing useful information so that they'll learn and grow. I also try to assess whether someone is asking for praise or asking for feedback. I'll gladly give either or both to them. Giving feedback to myself, I'm a little more blunt and straightforward.

Similarly to how I provided my younger-knitter-self feedback on the Arctic Sweater, I'd like to do the same thing for my initial efforts of knitting the fabric of the Men's Knitting Retreats community. Here's what I'd say to the younger me:

> *On a positive note, the fabric turned out spectacularly well. It is uniformly knit and intricate in the materials gathered and used. Without any experience in blending multiple, varied strands of personalities, you accomplished an impressive feat. Understanding how to hold the space in a way that allowed the group to coalesce and experience the joy of spontaneous community was particularly surprising for someone who is self-taught. Of particular note as well, is your creativity in making the experience a memorable one for the guys who attended. All quite astounding for a first-time community knitter.*
>
> *The first area of noticeable improvements you could have made was in your tensioning. The most obvious example of that is how tightly you felt you had to control various aspects of the group - roommates and housing for the guys, setting such a tight exacting agenda and dealing with the retreat center staff. All of those activities could have been looser. Also, an understanding of when to trust the process and the group of guys who attend needs some work. Realizing earlier in the process that each of the*

attendees knows better than you, which method of sewing them together will create the most stable and long-lasting fabric.

Finally, your reticence to rely on the support tools you had on-hand may have made the process longer than it needed to be. The co-coordinators, the retreat center staff and your allies are all amazing and you could have made the creation of this garment much easier if you had allowed them to support you. You chose to be too self-reliant and to not delegate responsibility, making it difficult for co-coordinators to learn and grow and at the same time your personal burden too dense and heavy. You may well be modeling the dictionary definition of "control-freak" to the attendees, the co-coordinators and the other regional coordinators.

Perhaps those last few critiques were a little less than helpful. But I can honestly admit that I have a lot of difficulty letting others participate in the production of these events and the administration of the logistical aspects of the Men's Knitting Retreats.

I will say that the initial retreat unwittingly put into place many foundational principles that have served us well over the years. The three primary principles of the retreat are:
1. The retreats should be for men only as a celebration of the men's knitting community.
2. The Men's Knitting Retreats are not-for-profit (and hopefully not-for-loss). Financially we try to break even on each event but the purpose is definitely not to profit financially from the retreats.

3. Expertise for workshops, demonstrations and expert tables should first be sought out from volunteers from our attendees to reduce the cost of hiring outside talent.

Being not-for-profit works well for a number of reasons. First, it ensures that the largest number of guys who want to, can more easily afford to attend. And second, eliminating a profit motive from our actions makes it much easier to establish a trusted relationship with the guys. Removing money from the equation as much as possible makes it easier for all of those involved, and makes it clear that each guy's participation is more important than their financial contribution to a retreat.

Asking participants to volunteer their expertise had some surprising impacts. For some of the guys who had never led a knitting workshop, it showed that we had a vast pool of talent and expertise in various fiber-arts. Many of our attendees had their first experience demonstrating a skill that they had never been asked to teach. There were some guys who attended, who made a living delivering knitting workshops, and yet they were very generous with offering to teach a workshop for a group they considered important. Both groups gained an enormous amount of satisfaction in how much they could contribute to this community.

Finally, having a space organized by men and for men turned out to be a key component of a strong knitting community. Especially since many of us identified as outsiders in the general knitting community, and we hadn't even known how much we had been yearning to coalesce. The celebratory experience of spending time with others with a common shared experience, that not many outside the community truly understood, was transformative for many of us.

Chapter 19
Creating An Heirloom

"You are being called to live a bigger life. Answer the call. Playing small does not serve you."

Les Brown

A knitted heirloom isn't simply an example of beauty and expertise in knitting. Yes, it is sometimes a combination of beauty and expertise, but it is also the thoughts evoked by a loved one who took the time to craft an extraordinary creation. It's the memory of an event that it was given to celebrate. And it's the loving use of the object which has imbued it forever with meaning and value. The heirloom could be a receiving blanket for a newborn, a fine-gauge lace shawl for a bride or even a lovingly crafted afghan for a niece or nephew's high school graduation. Whenever something knitted becomes cherished and beloved, it becomes an heirloom.

For a fiber-artist, there is no greater praise than having someone cherish something you've made for them so much that they pass it down to future generations.

When I first started living with Thaddeus, he had an afghan crocheted by his grandmother. It was a diagonally striped afghan done in colors from the 1960's - orange, tan, beige and brown, and it had a shell edging around the outer edge. Thaddeus loved this blanket because of all that it represented. It embodied the generation of his youth, the time and care taken on his behalf, and the love he had for his grandmother. Despite all that, he still considered this as a runner-up prize heirloom. He couldn't get the truly prized heirloom that his grandmother used to make for all of her grandchildren when they got married. His grandmother used to give a wedding gift of two handmade, down-filled pillows to her grandchildren. Thaddeus asked her once if he could get one of her cherished down pillows since he would never be able to get married. She declined the request saying that she only created pillows as wedding gifts. Unfortunately, she passed away years before we were legally able to get married. He was still grateful for the crocheted afghan as his inheritance from her.

Back in the early 2000's he asked me once if I could replicate the afghan in different colors. I knew how to crochet, but not as well as I knew how to knit and certainly not as well as his grandmother. I didn't know how she had made the afghan. I told him I'd be glad to try and unravel his afghan a little to see if I could figure it out. He nervously told me to go ahead, but not if there was any chance that I couldn't put it back together. It was simple to pull out the shell edging at the beginning corner of the afghan and I felt comfortable knowing that I could recreate those stitches. I could see where his grandmother had carefully woven in her yarn-ends to make sure they wouldn't come loose. I started to unravel the corner of the first diagonal stripe in the blanket and realized that I was quickly getting in over my head. I hastily re-finished the one stitch I had unraveled and crocheted the edging back in place. I also lovingly re-wove in the remaining yarn-ends to keep his heirloom intact.

Since then, with the abundance of information on the

internet, it has become much easier to reverse-engineer such an afghan. I did eventually find out the stitch that she used. It is called corner-to-corner stitch and it's a great method for crocheting different colored diagonal stripes. I have since been able to make a number of these diagonally striped blankets. But none of them has ever risen to the level of heirloom…yet. As a sign of his reverence for the item, Thaddeus recently brought the afghan to a family gathering to pass it down to one of the great-granddaughters. She was very grateful for the piece of family history.

Not all items that I make with great love and care become heirlooms. The additional qualities of being used and cherished by a grateful recipient and being seen as a quiet reminder of the person who made it, need to be there as well. And even then, an item might not reach heirloom status.

A few years ago, my mom asked me to knit her a cardigan. My mom is a petite woman who wears very smart and stylish looking clothes. She's more the Ann Taylor type than something more funky or trendy. I asked her to show me a cardigan she currently owned so I could take some measurements. As I expected, she brought out a conservatively stylish, fine-gauge sweater that could easily have been part of a twin-set. I took all the measurements and then found the perfect yarn to make the kind of fabric for her cardigan. It was a fine-gauge, soft wool in classic medium gray. I also found the perfect delicate buttons from a large collection of buttons that I've been curating over the years.

With a vision of what I wanted to make and all the materials, I started right away. I knit a small square using the selected yarn to check my gauge. Knowing how many stitches and rows in each inch of my test-swatch would let me get an accurate width and length to the finished garment. I cast on and designed the cardigan as I went. It was going to be a simple cropped cardigan with a round neckline and set-in sleeves.

Surprisingly, the sweater practically knit itself. I had no missteps and my efforts resulted in exactly the sweater I had imagined. I sewed it all together, sewed on the buttons and wove in all the yarn-ends and washed and blocked the sweater. Blocking is a term used for shaping a knitted fabric either using steam or by laying it out wet. Blocking makes hand knit stitches more even and uniform and gives a knitted garment its final shaping. This particular sweater looked almost commercially made, especially after blocking.

I gave it to my mom for Christmas in 2010 and she was as pleased as I was with the result. It fit her perfectly, looked fantastic on her and was exactly the weight of a sweater she was looking for to keep her from getting chilly inside or outside her house. She continues to wear it often.

Despite the fact that everything went exactly right with this project and my mom got a perfect sweater that she'll always cherish, it still most likely won't ever be an heirloom. Perhaps, as a functional garment, it just seems too ordinary, or maybe the petite sizing of the cardigan will be something that few people will be able to wear if it was passed down. There was still great satisfaction in making this garment. The satisfaction that only extreme care and love can bring to a project.

Creating an heirloom community has also been an extraordinarily satisfying venture.

Successfully supporting and encouraging this community to grow has been transformative for me and many of the people that have participated. I realized that much like the skills I developed for being able to create knitted fabric, I was also able to develop the skills to create the fabric of community.

One of my first lessons I learned as my community-building skills were in their early stages, was being highly supportive and encouraging of every level of effort. When it came to the retreats, this had an important impact on both the individual attendee and the groups who got to see it in action. The behavior of valuing each individual, quickly became the practice for everyone who witnessed it. It ended up being one of the unwritten core principles of the Men's Knitting Retreat community. The Show & Tell portion of the retreats was the part of the agenda that most clearly demonstrates how important it is to be encouraging of each other.

I've observed one other important, much less measurable skill that allows for a community to grow and thrive. The more successful regional coordinators of the retreat seem to have the ability to intuitively create a space where a community can form. For me, creating a space entails many components, such as building excitement prior to the event, creating logistics that make it easy to let the guys coalesce and grow as a group, being receptive to changes that make guys feel more eager to participate and constantly being mindful of the overall mood of the group and adjusting my efforts as necessary. One might think that being so deliberately mindful of a group of forty guys over four days might be draining. But I've found that it's quite the opposite. It's incredibly energizing when it's for a goal I value as much as this one.

When my body is no longer breathing and my heart no longer beats, the legacy of the community that I was able to help foster will be a living tribute to everything that went into it over the years that I was around. The enthusiastic participation and support of the guys who have participated in this community have fed the reverence and value that have helped this community be considered a true heirloom that I hope will be passed down for a long time to come.

The unwitting events that have led up to these retreats have taught me the importance of taking great care and deliberation in every new project that I start - even if it never becomes an heirloom. Whenever I put a lot of myself into something, I grow, regardless of whether the effort turns out perfectly or not. When my purpose is growth, even a bad outcome is at worst a learning experience. And for a project to result in something truly exceptional, there has to be great care taken. Approaching all new ventures with as much excellence as I can bring to it, at least provides for the possibility of an extraordinary outcome.

Earlier, in the Introduction of this book, I stated that I had no hidden agenda and that I didn't intend to persuade or sway you to think differently. That wasn't entirely true. Ideally, if my words influence you to take any part in a budding community that sparks your interest, then the legacy of all that the guys in the knitting world has created will have the ripple effect that was my true intention.

Epilogue
The Ripple Effect

The initial Men's Spring Knitting retreat rapidly expanded as it spawned regional retreats across the United States, as well as in Canada, the UK and New Zealand. But it also highlighted the existence of small groups of guys who knit, who had been getting together less formally to enjoy the company of like-minded fellows. Southern California had a small group of guys who scheduled regular annual trips to varying cabins or lodges in different natural venues in their beautiful State. There were a few unofficial groups of guys who met regularly in places like Provincetown, New York City or Seattle just to be able to spend time among their peers.

It was incredibly satisfying when someone who attended the retreat got to experience the wonder of becoming part of the community. It was even more satisfying when they felt so inspired, that they went out and replicated that experience with others.

At the Spring retreat in 2018 in Upstate NY, a guy from New York City attended the retreat for the first time. Doug and his husband were slated to move to Palm Springs on the weekend of the MSKR and he rescheduled their move so that he could be at the retreat. Like many before him, he contributed an enormous amount to the community and was deeply moved by the experience. The rescheduled relocation to Palm Springs occurred the following weekend. In addition to all of their belongings and their dog, Cooper, Doug took with him the experience of the wondrous community at the retreat. Once life got a little settled for him, Doug started his own knitting group, which also spawned the virtual meetings that spanned the times during COVID. Doug still comes back to the East Coast for the Men's Spring Knitting Retreat and tells me often the impact his initial experience of the knitting community has had in his new home State. The stories of the family that he has built up and their amazing commitment to each other has been inspiring.

Currently, there are seven regional Men's Knitting Retreats regularly scheduled on an annual basis. There are two retreats in Upstate New York, one in the Spring and one in the Fall, the Rocky Mountain retreat near Estes Park, Colorado, the Southeast retreat in North Carolina near Asheville, the Great Lakes retreat in Michigan, the Pacific Northwest retreat near Seattle and a touring Men's Knitting Retreat with a changing venue of cruise ships and land tours. They are all organized and coordinated by volunteers from within our community - guys who felt compelled to share their experience of joy and camaraderie and the strong bond of the fabric of community. There is also an overarching, umbrella organization which maintains the web site, and email list of guys who want to be notified when a retreat opens for registration.

The spark of enthusiasm generated by my friend's description of knitting socks has resulted in a glorious stitch pattern of men in loving and supportive communities. I'm grateful every time I get to participate in these groups, as it reminds me of the wandering journey that brought me here, and all the exceptional people who helped make it happen.

Acknowledgments

Many thanks to Lisa Stolzer for both encouraging me to document the pattern for this extraordinary community and also all her help in editing and writing skills. A huge thank-you to all of the regional coordinators and co-coordinators of the various Men's Knitting Retreats who have taken a kernel of an idea and made it extraordinary. You are an exceptional group of guys that I am blessed to be considered a part of. Also, thanks to all the staff and volunteers at Easton Mountain who have supported our retreats with as much passion and love as we do. Finally, much love and gratitude to my husband, Thaddeus for supporting me and giving me the freedom to pursue all that I've become.

www.ingramcontent.com/pod-product-compliance
Lightning Source LLC
LaVergne TN
LVHW021959060526
838201LV00048B/1623